Hands-On Activities   With Scripture Values

LEVEL **G**

STUDENT WORKTEXT

ISBN #1-58938-146-7
Published by The Concerned Group, Inc.
700 East Granite • PO Box 1000 • Siloam Springs, AR 72761

Authors	**Dave & Rozann Seela**
Publisher	**Russ L. Potter, II**
Senior Editor	**Bill Morelan**
Project Coordinator	**Rocki Vanatta**
Creative Director	**Daniel Potter**
Proofreader	**Elizabeth Granderson**
Step Illustrations	**Steven Butler**
Character Illustrations	**Josh Ray**
Colorists	**Josh & Aimee Ray**

Printed on recycled paper in the United States

For more information about **A Reason For**® curricula,
write to the address above, call, or visit our website.

www.areasonfor.com
800.447.4332

Dear Parent,

Welcome to a new school year! This letter is to introduce you to **A Reason For©** Science.

A Reason For© Science teaches basic Life, Earth, and Physical Science through fun, hands-on activities. Each lesson is tied directly to the **National Science Education Content Standards** and uses an inquiry-based approach designed to enhance learning.

Today's increasingly complex world requires a clear understanding of science and technology. Our future prosperity depends on helping children rediscover the challenges, excitement, and joy of science — especially in the context of Scripture values. Thus, one of the primary goals of **A Reason For©** Science is to make science not only meaningful, but also FUN!

Fun, Flexible Format
Instead of a hardback textbook filled with "facts" to memorize, your child will be working in an interactive worktext designed to develop critical-thinking skills. Students start each week with a hands-on activity demonstrating a key science concept. This is followed by group discussion, journaling, and a series of thought-provoking questions. Lessons conclude with a summary of key concepts and a related "object lesson" from Scripture.

Safety Issues
The hands-on nature of **A Reason For©** Science means your child will be working with age-appropriate materials. (For instance, the "acids" we use are actually dilute forms comparable to typical household chemicals.) Like a field trip or gym class, these science activities usually require simple safety precautions.

But for instructional reasons, all materials in **A Reason For©** Science are treated as hazardous! This encourages students to develop good safety habits for use in later years. (If you have further questions about safety, your child's teacher has an in-depth safety manual outlining precautions for every lesson.)

Scripture Values
Best of all, **A Reason For©** Science features Scripture values! Every lesson concludes with a Scripture object lesson related to the week's topic. These "Food for Thought" sections encourage students to relate everyday experiences to Scriptural themes, providing a positive way to integrate faith and learning.

Here's to an exciting year exploring God's world!

Dave & Rozann Seela
Authors, **A Reason For©** Science

EXPLORING GOD'S WORLD! Science

A Reason For© Science makes science FUN! Your school year will be filled with hands-on activities, colorful discovery sheets, and lots of discussion and exploration. You'll discover many exciting new things as you explore God's world!

Although "almost everything relates to everything else" in some way or another, scientists usually divide science into three broad areas for study: **life**, **earth,** and **physical science**. The sections in your worktext are based on these categories.

Colorful icons are used to help you identify each section. An **ant** represents **Life Science** lessons. A **globe** stands for **Earth Science** lessons. An **atom** introduces **Physical Science (Energy/Matter)** lessons. And a **hammer** represents the **Physical Science (Forces)** lessons.

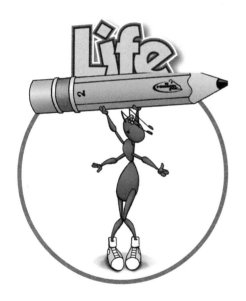

Life Science

Life Science is the study of **living things.** In the Life Science section of your **A Reason For©** Science worktext, you'll explore different kinds of living things. You'll learn about their characteristics (how they're alike or different). You'll discover how scientists classify (label and sort) living things. You'll even learn more about your own body and how it works!

Earth Science

Earth Science is the study of **earth** and **sky**. In the Earth Science section of your **A Reason For©** Science worktext, you'll explore the structure of our planet (rocks, crystals, volcanos), the atmosphere (air, clouds), and related systems (water cycles, air pressure, weather). Grades 7 and 8 reach out even further with a look at the solar system and stars.

Physical Science

Physical Science is the study of **energy, matter,** and related **forces.** Since the physical part of science has a big effect on your daily life, it's divided into two major sections:

Energy and Matter

In this section of your **A Reason For©** Science worktext, you'll learn about the different **states** and unique **properties** of **matter**. You'll discover new things about light and sound. You'll explore physical and chemical reactions. Some grades will explore related concepts like circuits, currents, and convection.

Forces

In this section of your **A Reason For©** Science worktext, you'll discover how "**push** and **pull**" form the basis for all physical movement. You'll explore simple machines (levers, pulleys). You'll work with Newton's laws of motion. You'll even learn to understand concepts like torque, inertia, and buoyancy.

Safety First!

Before you begin, be sure to read about "Peat" the safety worm. Peat's job is to warn you whenever there's a potential hazard around. (Whenever you see Peat and his warning sign, STOP and wait for further instructions from your teacher!)

Exploring God's world of science often requires using equipment or materials that can injure you if they're not handled correctly. Also, many accidents occur when people hurry, are careless, or ignore safety rules.

It's your responsibility to know and observe the rules and to use care and caution as you work. Just like when you're on the playground, horseplay or ignoring safety rules can be dangerous. Don't let an accident happen to you!

Meet "Peat" the Safety Worm!

Peat's job is to warn you whenever there's a potential hazard around. Whenever you see Peat and his warning sign, **STOP** and wait for further instructions from your teacher!

Peat's sign helps you know what kind of hazard is present. Before beginning each activity, your teacher will discuss this hazard in detail and review the safety rules that apply.

means this activity requires **PROTECTIVE GEAR.**

Usually **gloves** or **goggles** (or both) are required. Goggles protect your eyes from things like flying debris or splashing liquids. Gloves protect your hands from things like heat, broken glass, or corrosive chemicals.

means there is a BURN HAZARD. There are three common burn hazards.

"Open Flame" indicates the presence of fire (often matches or a candle). "Thermal Burn" means objects may be too hot to touch. "Corrosion" indicates a chemical substance is present.

means there is a POISON HAZARD.

There are three common poison hazards. "Skin Contact" indicates a substance that should not touch skin. "Vapor" indicates fumes that should not be inhaled. "Hygiene" indicates the presence of materials that may contain germs.

indicates OTHER HAZARDS.

There are three additional hazards that require caution. "Breakage" indicates the presence of fragile substances (like glass). "Slipping" indicates liquids that might spill on the floor. "Sharp Objects" indicates the presence of tools with sharp edges or points.

Play It Safe!

Exploring God's world with **A Reason For©** Science can be great fun, but remember — play it safe! Observe all the safety rules, handle equipment and materials carefully, and always be cautious and alert.

And don't forget Peat the safety worm! Whenever you see Peat and his warning sign, **STOP** and wait for further instructions from your teacher.

Life

LESSONS 1-9

Life Science

Life Science is the study of **living things.** In this section, you'll explore different kinds of living things. You'll learn about their characteristics (how they're alike or different). You'll discover how scientists classify (label and sort) living things. You'll even learn more about your own body and how it works!

NAME _____

SURVIVOR SEEDS

FOCUS   Respiration

OBJECTIVE   To explore how seeds use energy and oxygen

OVERVIEW   You probably know that plants produce oxygen for us to breathe. But did you know plants use oxygen, too? In this activity, we'll make a simple device to prove this.

WHAT TO DO

STEP 1

Cut the large bulb off the pipette, then **cut** the two small sections off the other end. **Insert** what's left (a straight tube about three inches long) into the one-hole stopper. **Leave** about 1/2 inch sticking out of the wide end.

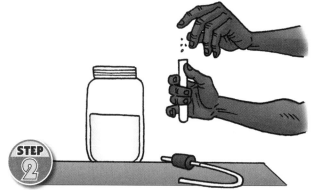

STEP 2

Pour one inch of seeds into the large test tube. **Wet** the seeds thoroughly. **Attach** the clear hose to the short end of the pipette tube, then **push** the stopper into the test tube. **Fill** a small jar about half full of water.

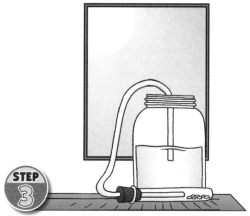

STEP 3

Move your materials to a warm place with plenty of sunlight. **Lay** the test tube beside the jar, then **place** the hose in the water. (Tape if needed.) **Record** what happens to the seeds and the water in the tube.

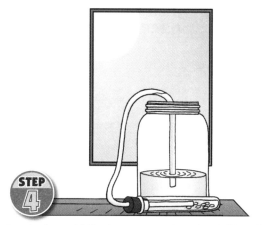

STEP 4

[end of week] **Review** your notes about Step 3 changes. **Discuss** what happened to the water in the tube. **Predict** why this might have happened. **Share** and **compare** observations with other research teams.

WHAT HAPPENED?

When conditions are right, seeds can **germinate** (sprout). That's what happened in this activity! Using the **food energy** stored in the main part of the seed, the **embryo** (baby plant) began to sprout.

But sprouting **seeds** need a lot of **oxygen** to grow. As the seeds used up the oxygen trapped in the test tube, there was less air, resulting in lower **air pressure**. This created a small **vacuum** that **pulled** water from the jar into the test tube.

As the seed begins to grow into a full-size plant, the chemical **chlorophyll** (which makes plants look green) starts the **photosynthesis** process. The plant begins converting **carbon dioxide** into oxygen, making much more oxygen than the plant needs. But as you can see from this activity, young seeds need a lot of oxygen in order to get to that point!

WHAT WE LEARNED

1 **What was the only way anything could get into the test tube after Step 2? Why was this "closed system" important?**

_____

_____

_____

_____

_____

_____

_____

2 **Why was it important to place the test tube in a warm place with plenty of light? What effect might it have had on the activity if you'd placed the test tube in a dark, cool closet?**

_____

_____

_____

_____

_____

_____

3 Describe changes that occurred by the end of the week. How did the seeds look? What happened to water levels in the jar and test tube?

_____

_____

_____

_____

_____

_____

4 Compare a plant's needs during the germination stage with its needs at maturity. How are they similar? How are they different?

_____

_____

_____

_____

_____

_____

5 Based on what you've learned, would it be easier to breathe in an airtight room full of sprouting seeds or mature plants? Explain your answer.

_____

_____

_____

_____

_____

_____

CONCLUSION

Seeds are alive. As seeds germinate and begin to grow into plants, they require a lot of oxygen. When plants mature, they give off more oxygen than they use.

FOOD FOR THOUGHT

Genesis 1:29 Although hard, dry seeds look completely dead, they're really a storehouse full of life! Seeds are the primary source of food on Earth — for both humans and livestock. Take away seeds, and everyone starves.

This Scripture reminds us that seed-bearing plants are a gift from God. Our wondrous world is filled with an abundance of wonderful life-giving plants. Yet all too often, mankind abuses this gift, and large areas become barren and wasted. Maintaining a balanced ecology means developing good habits. Recycle, don't pollute, don't litter. Look for ways in your community to apply these ideas!

JOURNAL My Science Notes

_____

_____

_____

_____

_____

_____

_____

_____

_____

_____

_____

_____

_____

_____

_____

_____

_____

_____

APPLE EMBRYO

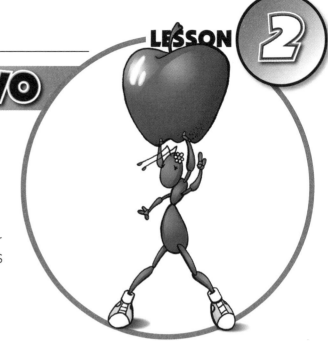

FOCUS   Plant Reproduction

OBJECTIVE   To explore how plants reproduce

OVERVIEW   We usually just think of apples as something to eat. But what is the real purpose of an apple — at least as far as an apple tree is concerned? In this activity, we'll take a closer look.

WHAT TO DO

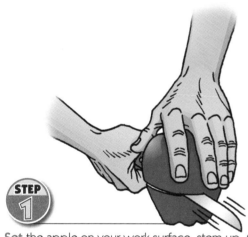

STEP 1

Set the apple on your work surface, stem up. Carefully **cut** the apple in half horizontally. **Pick up** the half with the stem and **cover** the cut face with lemon juice. **Set** both halves aside to dry until tomorrow.

STEP 2

[next day] **Compare** the two apple halves, and **make notes** about similarities and differences. **Draw** an apple face, paying close attention to the center section and the outer edges. **Color** if desired.

STEP 3

Closely **observe** the "star" in the center of the apple. **Remove** and **count** the seeds. Now carefully **cut** a seed in half. **Make notes** about everything you observe. **Clean up** as directed by your teacher.

STEP 4

Review each step in this activity. **Make notes** describing the parts of the apple (skin, flesh, seeds) and the proportions of each. **Share** and **compare** observations with your research team.

WHAT HAPPENED?

An apple is really a storehouse for a baby apple tree (**embryo**)! The part we like to eat provides **food** for the **seeds** until they **sprout** and put out **roots** and **leaves**. When an apple falls to the ground, it soon begins to **decompose** (rot). You saw a glimpse of this in Step 1 when the untreated face began to turn brown. **Enzymes** were already beginning to break down the apple's **cells**. Lemon juice provided a coating of **acid** on the treated apple face to slow this process down.

Pollination is the first step in making an apple. **Pollen** from the **male** part of a **flower** has to get to the **female** part. If two flowers are involved, the process is called **cross-pollination**. Some flowers that have both male and female parts **self-pollinate**. Pollination requires some kind of assistance in order to occur. A light breeze provides one common method, and bees provide another.

WHAT WE LEARNED

1 Compare the treated and untreated apple faces from Step 2.
How were they similar? How were they different?

_____

_____

_____

_____

_____

_____

_____

2 What caused the color change on the untreated apple face?
How is this process helpful in nature?

_____

_____

_____

_____

_____

_____

_____

3 What is the purpose of the white material (the main part of the apple)? How does it help seeds grow?

_____

_____

_____

_____

_____

_____

4 Explain the difference between cross-pollination and self-pollination.

_____

_____

_____

_____

_____

_____

5 How does an apple edibility contribute to the propagation of apple trees? Over time, what might happen if apples weren't carried away?

_____

_____

_____

_____

_____

_____

CONCLUSION

In some plants, pollination creates fruit. The fruit provides an energy source for the growing seeds. The edibility of fruit helps scatter seeds away from the parent plant.

FOOD FOR THOUGHT

Matthew 7:15-20 When you see apples growing on a tree, you can be sure it's an apple tree! Jesus used this idea to illustrate how we can tell what people are really like inside. If someone pretends to be beautiful, but doesn't treat others kindly, we know they aren't what they seem.

Whenever we try to pretend we're good but don't spend time getting to know God, our actions eventually give us away. The closer we get to God, the more we'll reflect his goodness and character. As God fills us with his love, we begin to bear "fruit" (see Galatians 5:22) that shows what we're really like inside.

JOURNAL My Science Notes

PYRIC PEANUT

FOCUS   Food Energy

OBJECTIVE   To discover that energy is stored in food

OVERVIEW   No one likes to miss a meal — we get hungry! Why do our bodies need food? In this activity, we'll explore the importance of food and what food actually does.

WHAT TO DO

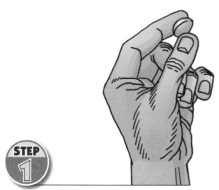

STEP 1

Pick up your peanut. **Remove** the shell and red husk so you have a bare, light brown seed. **Rub** the peanut gently between your index finger and thumb. **Make notes** about what you feel.

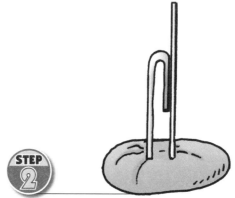

STEP 2

Mold a piece of clay into a ball about the size of a quarter. **Place** it on your work surface and **flatten** it slightly. **Bend** one end of a paper clip straight out to make a tiny "spear." **Push** the rounded end into the clay.

STEP 3

Attach the peanut to the paperclip with a pinch of clay. Now **light** the match and **hold** it under the end of the peanut. **Record** the results. **Clean up** as directed by your teacher.

STEP 4

Now **review** each step in this activity. **Make notes** about what you observed and why you think it happened. **Share** and **compare** observations with other research teams.

WHAT HAPPENED?

Peanuts have a lot of **oil** (fat) stored inside. When you set the oil on fire (**combustion**), it resulted in **light** and **heat**. This is a great example of the **transfer of energy**. The process of combustion converted the energy from **potential energy** to heat — a form of **kinetic** (moving) **energy**.

Your body does a great job of changing food energy (**calories**) into an energy form you can use. Within your body, calories are converted into all kinds of energy: the warmth of your body (**heat** energy); your brain signaling your muscles (**electrical** energy); your muscles moving to perform work (**mechanical** energy).

Remember, your body can only process what you put into it. For optimum efficiency, you should avoid foods with "empty" calories (like junk food), and feed your body the right kinds of foods.

WHAT WE LEARNED

1 **Describe the feel of the seed in Step 1. What material causes this slippery feeling?**

2 **Explain the combustion process that took place in Step 3. Why did the peanut burn? How did this demonstrate energy conversion?**

3 Compare burning a peanut to eating a peanut. In terms of energy production, how are they similar? How are they different?

_____

_____

_____

_____

_____

_____

_____

4 What would happen if your body quit converting food energy? How can diet affect how well your body processes food?

_____

_____

_____

_____

_____

_____

_____

5 Do all foods contain the same amount of energy? Give some examples and explain your answer.

_____

_____

_____

_____

_____

_____

_____

CONCLUSION

Food contains energy. Your body converts food into the energy forms we need for life. Some foods work better for this process than others.

FOOD FOR THOUGHT

Matthew 25; 1-13 Peanuts are full of tasty calories that come in the form of oil. This oil is what made the peanut burn so well. Proper food is essential. It's never a good idea to run out of fuel — whether it's calories for your body, gas for your car, or spiritual food for your soul!

This Scripture talks about some foolish girls who didn't prepare and ran out of fuel. Instead of filling their lamps that day, they tried to rely on leftover oil. How about your "fuel" supply? Are you relying on leftovers, or are you "filling your lamp" with the love of Jesus every day?

JOURNAL   My Science Notes

_____
_____
_____
_____
_____
_____
_____
_____
_____
_____
_____
_____
_____
_____
_____
_____
_____
_____

NAME _____

STARCH SEARCH

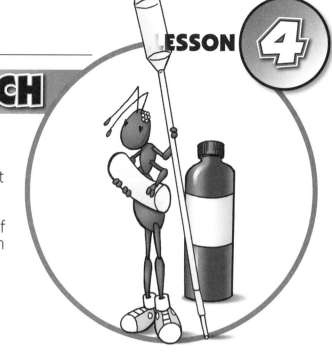

FOCUS Nutrients

OBJECTIVE To explore testing food for a nutrient

OVERVIEW Food contains a lot of energy, and nutrients are one important source of this energy. In this activity, we'll learn how to test food for a key nutrient.

WHAT TO DO

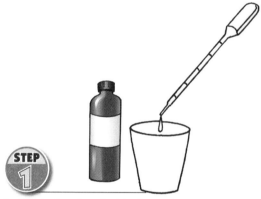

STEP 1

Iodine is the chemical indicator in this activity since it turns a deep purple or black in the presence of starch (an important nutrient). **Pour** some water in a paper cup. **Add** three drops of iodine. **Record** the results. **Dispose** of the iodine as directed by your teacher. (Do this after every step!)

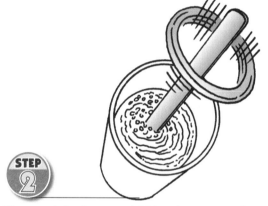

STEP 2

Rinse and **dry** the cup. **Add** two teaspoons of water. **Drop** in a corn-based packing peanut and **stir** until completely dissolved. (If it's too thick, add a little more water.) Now **add** three drops of iodine. **Record** the results.

STEP 3

Rinse and **dry** the cup. **Add** two teaspoons of water, then one teaspoon of sugar. **Stir** until completely dissolved. Now **add** three drops of iodine. **Record** the results.

STEP 4

Rinse and **dry** the cup. Now **repeat** Step 3 using flour instead of sugar. **Record** the results. **Review** each step in this activity. **Share** and **compare** observations with other research teams.

WHAT HAPPENED?

Food contains **energy**. **Nutrients** are one form of this energy. Key nutrients include **proteins**, **vitamins**, **minerals**, **fats**, **sugars**, and **starches**. Sugars and starches are a group of nutrients called **carbohydrates**. The name describes a combination of the **elements** carbon (carbo) and water (hydrate).

The packing peanuts we used are made from corn starch. Since iodine changes colors in the presence of starch, the corn starch solution turned deep purple.

Although you may have seen **petroleum**-based packing pellets made from materials like Styrofoam®, many companies are switching to the starch-based material. Unlike petroleum oil, corn (the source of this material) is a **renewable resource** — one that can be grown and even **recycled**.

WHAT WE LEARNED

1 Describe what happened when you added the iodine to the solution in Step 2.

_____

_____

_____

_____

_____

_____

_____

2 Describe what happened when you added the iodine to the solution in Step 3.

_____

_____

_____

_____

_____

_____

_____

3 Describe what happened when you added the iodine to the solution in Step 4.

_____

_____

_____

_____

_____

_____

4 Name at least three nutrients. What is the group of nutrients containing sugar and starch called?

_____

_____

_____

_____

_____

_____

5 Explain the difference between the packing peanuts we used and Styrofoam® peanuts. Which is more environmentally friendly? Why?

_____

_____

_____

_____

_____

_____

_____

CONCLUSION

Food contains energy. Nutrients are one form of this energy. The presence of one nutrient (starch) can be determined by using an iodine solution as an indicator.

FOOD FOR THOUGHT

Psalm 139:23-24 It wasn't hard to tell that starch was present. The color change was dramatic! And no matter what kind of food the starch is in, or how hard it is to see, this test will still give you an indication that it's there.

In this Scripture, David is asking God to perform a kind of indicator test on his soul. He wants to know if there is anything inside him that might displease God. He wants God to help him get rid of any trace of evil in his life.

You can pray this same prayer. The more your heart is filled with the good things that come from Jesus, the less room there is for the bad things that come from sin.

JOURNAL My Science Notes

SEALED CELL

FOCUS Diffusion

OBJECTIVE To explore how materials pass through a cell's membrane

OVERVIEW The cell is a basic building block for living things. In this activity, we'll model how materials move in and out of cells to keep them healthy.

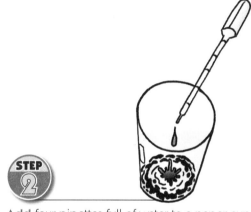

WHAT TO DO

STEP 1

Tie a string tightly around one end of the casing. **Soak** the casing in warm water so you can open the other end. (This may take several minutes. Be patient.) **Complete** Step 2 while you're waiting.

STEP 2

Add four pipettes full of water to a paper cup. **Stir** in one tablespoon of cornstarch. **Add** a few drops of this solution to a clear plastic cup. Now **add** a few drops of iodine. **Record** the results, then **rinse** the cup thoroughly.

STEP 3

Pour the starch solution into the casing and **tie off** the end to seal it. **Wash** your new "cell" carefully. Now **fill** the clear cup two thirds full of water. **Stir** in two pipettes of iodine, then **slip** the sealed casing gently into the water.

STEP 4

Check your "cell" every few minutes until you see a change. Be patient! **Record** the results and **make notes** about what might have happened. **Share** and **compare** observations with other research teams.

WHAT HAPPENED?

As you discovered in Lesson 4, this color change is the result of a **chemical reaction** between **starch** and **iodine**. But how did the two get together? The starch was inside the casing, but the iodine was outside!

The secret lies in the material that the casing is made from. Although it looks like water-tight plastic, it actually behaves much like a living cell's **membrane**, letting tiny particles pass in and out in a process called **diffusion**. Diffusion keeps cells healthy by letting **oxygen** and **nutrients** in, and letting **waste** products out.

Why didn't the starch diffuse out as the iodine diffused in? It's because starch particles are much larger, made from hundreds of **sugar molecules** hooked together end to end. The starch particles were much too big to pass through the **Sealed Cell**'s membrane like the tiny iodine particles did.

WHAT WE LEARNED

1 What happened in the clear cup in Step 2? Why did this occur?

_____

_____

_____

_____

_____

_____

2 What living thing was modeled by the filled and tied casing in Step 3? How was the model similar? How was it different?

_____

_____

_____

_____

_____

_____

3 Describe what happened in Step 4. Explain why this occurred.

_____

_____

_____

_____

_____

_____

4 What is the name of the process by which materials pass through the cell membrane? How did this process differ between the iodine and the starch in Step 4? Why?

_____

_____

_____

_____

_____

_____

5 Based on what you've learned, do all substances have equal access to a cell's interior? Why or why not?

_____

_____

_____

_____

_____

_____

_____

CONCLUSION

Materials pass though the cell membrane in a process called diffusion. Diffusion may vary depending on the substance. Diffusion helps keep cells healthy and alive.

FOOD FOR THOUGHT

Genesis 28:12 The purpose of the membrane is to keep a cell alive. The membrane lets the cell exchange materials back and forth across its boundary, keeping the cell alive and healthy. If this exchange ceases, the cell will die.

This Scripture tells of Jacob's dream about a ladder between Earth and Heaven. Angels constantly went up and down the ladder — perhaps an illustration of taking prayers up to God and bringing God's blessings down to his people. Regardless of the symbolism, the exchange between God and man is vital. God's love is what keeps us alive, and whether we recognize it or not, we are dependent on God's constant care to survive.

JOURNAL   My Science Notes

NAME _____

BEADS OF BLOOD

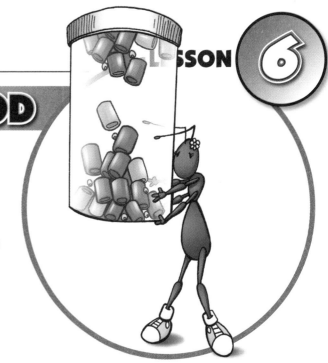

FOCUS Blood

OBJECTIVE To explore blood composition

OVERVIEW Ever wonder what makes up that fantastic fluid that flows through your veins (and arteries, too)? In this activity, we'll explore the composition of blood by making a model.

WHAT TO DO

STEP 1

Pour the bag of large red beads into the plastic jar. Now carefully **examine** the small bag of "mixed" beads. **Make notes** about quantities, shapes, and colors. **Pour** this bag of beads into the jar with the red beads.

STEP 2

Pour the bag of tiny orange beads into the jar. Slowly **fill** the jar with water and **fasten** the lid on firmly. **Dry** the outside of the jar carefully, then **shake** the jar to thoroughly mix the beads.

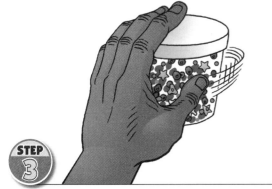

STEP 3

Hold the jar in one hand and **swirl** it gently. **Watch** the beads as they slowly spin. **Make notes** about what you see. **Predict** what each type of bead might represent (hint: check bag labels).

STEP 4

Carefully **pour** the water out of the jar. **Sort** and **dry** beads as directed by your teacher. Now **review** each step in this activity. **Share** and **compare** observations with your research team.

WHAT HAPPENED?

Here's what the parts of your **model** represent: First, human **blood** is primarily a water-based **liquid** called **plasma** (represented by water). Plasma contains dissolved **nutrients, waste products, gasses** like carbon dioxide and oxygen, disease-fighting chemicals called **antibodies**, chemical messengers called **hormones**, and many other substances. Plasma also moves **heat** to warm up or cool down the body.

Second are the **red blood cells** (represented by the red beads) called **erythrocytes**. They get their color from the **hemoglobin** they contain. This iron-rich chemical helps carry oxygen. Next are the **white blood cells** (represented by the other colored beads) called **leukocytes**. It's their job to fight **disease**! There are five different types of leukocytes. Finally come small, specialized cells (represented by the tiny beads) called **platelets**. These important cells cause blood to **clot** during an injury, preventing the loss of life-sustaining fluid!

WHAT WE LEARNED

1 What does the water in your model represent?
Describe the purpose of this blood part.

_____

_____

_____

_____

_____

_____

2 What do the red beads in your model represent?
Describe the purpose of this blood part.

_____

_____

_____

_____

_____

_____

_____

3 What do the other colored beads in your model represent?
Describe the purpose of this blood part.

_____

_____

_____

_____

_____

_____

4 What do the tiny beads in your model represent?
Describe the purpose of this blood part.

_____

_____

_____

_____

_____

_____

5 Name at least three of the substances that plasma contains.

_____

_____

_____

_____

_____

_____

_____

CONCLUSION

Human blood is a complex mixture of cells and liquids whose individual parts perform important functions in our bodies.

FOOD FOR THOUGHT

Mark 14:24 Human blood is a fantastic fluid that is tremendously complicated. When you are ill, it's one of the first places doctors check because it tells so much about what's going on inside your body. The importance of healthy blood to a human survival cannot be over-emphasized.

The most important blood in the Universe is the blood of Jesus. God's innocent son shed his blood in a violent, brutal crucifixion to ensure our salvation. Because of Jesus' sacrifice, we are offered the chance to live forever. What a marvelous symbol of God's enduring love!

JOURNAL My Science Notes

_____

_____

_____

_____

_____

_____

_____

_____

_____

_____

_____

_____

_____

_____

_____

_____

_____

_____

_____

_____

NAME _____

PREDATOR OR PREY

FOCUS Classification

OBJECTIVE To classify animals by eye location

OVERVIEW Scientists classify (sort) animals by their characteristics. The eyes of most predator animals are different from the eyes of prey animals. In this activity, we'll find out how.

WHAT TO DO

STEP 1

Remove the **Predator or Prey** page from the back of your worktext. **Cut** out all the animals. With your research team, **sort** the animals into groups according to various characteristics. **Record** the results.

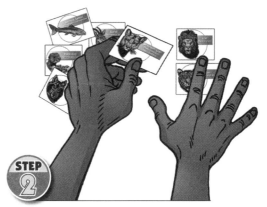

STEP 2

Place the animals back in a pile and start again. This time, **sort** them according to eye location only. Animals with eyes toward the side of the head (able to see both sides at once) go in one group. Animals with eyes on the front of the head (primarily forward vision) go in the other.

STEP 3

Write the word "dinner" on one sheet of paper, and the word "diner" on another. **Glue** prey animals (side vision) on the dinner sheet. **Glue** predator animals (forward vision) on the diner sheet.

STEP 4

Review each step in this activity. In your journal, **make notes** about why eye location is important and why it's one characteristic of these groups. **Share** and **compare** observations with other research teams.

LESSON D7

WHAT HAPPENED?

Just like a scientist, you sorted the animals into groups based on a specific **characteristic**. This process is called **classification**. Animals in the dinner group are often eaten by other animals. We call these animals **prey**. Animals in the diner group eat other animals. This kind of animal is called a **predator**. Such classifications make it easier for scientists to study different creatures.

Eyes located in front make it easier for predators to spot and follow a potential meal. Eyes on the side allow prey animals to watch a much wider area around them without turning their heads. This helps them spot potential danger much sooner, giving them a chance to avoid becoming someone's lunch!

WHAT WE LEARNED

1 What classification system did you use in Step 1?
How was this similar to Step 2? How was it different?

_____

_____

_____

_____

_____

_____

_____

2 Describe the eye location of most predators.
How does this contribute to their survival?

_____

_____

_____

_____

_____

_____

_____

3 Describe the eye location of most prey animals.
How does this contribute to their survival?

_____

_____

_____

_____

_____

_____

4 What is another name for "scientific sorting"?
How does such organization help scientists?

_____

_____

_____

_____

_____

_____

5 Based on what you've learned, classify the following animals:
a horse, a dog, a rabbit, a cat. Explain your answers.

_____

_____

_____

_____

_____

_____

CONCLUSION

Sorting animals into groups based on specific characteristics is called classification. Such organization makes it easier for scientists to study different kinds of creatures.

FOOD FOR THOUGHT

1 Peter 5:8 In this activity, we learned about predators and prey. Prey animals must remain constantly alert and pay close attention to their surroundings if they want to survive. Eye location can help them do this.

Scripture warns us of another kind of predator. Peter reminds us that Satan is constantly prowling around like a hungry lion, looking for some victim to tear apart. Staying close to Jesus helps us develop the spiritual eyes we need to keep us alert to danger. By trusting in God's power, we can stay safe from harm.

JOURNAL My Science Notes

_____

_____

_____

_____

_____

_____

_____

_____

_____

_____

_____

_____

_____

_____

_____

_____

_____

_____

_____

SPINDLY SPINE

FOCUS Human Anatomy

OBJECTIVE To explore the structure of the spine

OVERVIEW Everybody has a spine (backbone). How does this amazing body part work and what does it do? In this activity, we'll explore the spine by making a model!

WHAT TO DO

STEP 1

Working with your team members, **cut** tissue or paper towel tubes into 3/4 inch slices (thirty-three total). Use a paper punch to **punch** two holes in each slice. Now **cut** foam rubber into one-inch squares (thirty-two total).

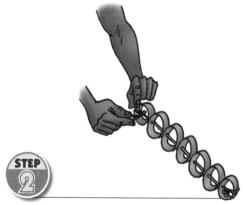

STEP 2

Tie (loop) ten rubber bands together end-to-end to make a rope. Carefully **thread** this rope through both holes in each cardboard slice. **Secure** the ends by looping them back over the end slice. **Record** the results so far.

STEP 3

Cut a slit in each foam rubber square. **Push** it onto the rubber band between the slices. Now **wrap** a pipe cleaner around the rubber band next to each piece of foam. **Spread** the ends out and up to each side like wings.

STEP 4

Hold up your **Spindly Spine** and **move** it around gently. **Make notes** about what you see. **Predict** what each part represents. **Share** and **compare** observations with other research teams.

WHAT HAPPENED?

You just made a **model** of your **spine**! Although it's sometimes called the **backbone**, the spine is not one bone but 33 individual bones called **vertebrae** (represented by the cardboard tubes). A large, thick **nerve** called the **spinal cord** (represented by the rubber band) runs from your **brain** down through the middle of these vertebrae. There are also areas of protective padding called **cartilage** (represented by the foam rubber). This is the same material that forms your nose and ears. Small **spinal nerves** (represented by the pipe cleaners) branch off the spinal cord. They help send information back and forth to your brain.

Even though its a very complex system, your spine is amazingly strong. It not only supports your entire body, but it's also flexible enough to let your body move in many different ways.

WHAT WE LEARNED

1 Describe the body structure represented by the cardboard tubes. What does this structure do?

_____

_____

_____

_____

_____

_____

_____

2 Describe the body structure represented by the rubber band. What does this structure do?

_____

_____

_____

_____

_____

_____

_____

3 Describe the body structure represented by the foam rubber pieces. What do these structures do?

_____

_____

_____

_____

_____

_____

4 Describe the body structure represented by the pipe cleaners. What do these structures do?

_____

_____

_____

_____

_____

_____

5 If your spinal cord was damaged, interrupting the flow of information from the spinal nerves to the brain, what might happen to the body structures below the damaged area?

_____

_____

_____

_____

_____

_____

_____

? CONCLUSION

Your spine (backbone) protects your spinal cord, supports your body, and provides channels for information to flow between your brain and the rest of your body.

FOOD FOR THOUGHT

Genesis 1:20-30 Making this model helped you see the incredible complexity of the human spine. Yet this model represents only one part of a human body. Imagine making models of all the human body parts — or modeling all the parts of all the animals that ever lived! Now that's complex!

It's mind-boggling to think about the incredible complexity God dealt with during creation. The first chapter of Genesis talks about the fantastic forms of life God created. Can you imagine what went into designing and making even one species of animal? What a marvelous God we serve! Take time this week to thank God for all the wonderful things he has made.

JOURNAL   My Science Notes

_____

_____

_____

_____

_____

_____

_____

_____

_____

_____

_____

_____

_____

_____

_____

_____

_____

_____

_____

_____

_____

_____

EXPERIMENTAL EPIDEMIC

FOCUS Disease Transmission

OBJECTIVE To explore how disease can spread so fast and far

OVERVIEW Diseases sometimes spread rapidly across vast areas. How do they travel so fast? In this activity, we'll model the process with a little chemistry.

WHAT TO DO

STEP 1

Use a marking pen to **write** Index Case on a clear plastic cup. Now **label** three paper cups A, B, and C, then **label** five paper cups 1, 2, 3, 4, and 5. **Fill** all nine cups half full of water.

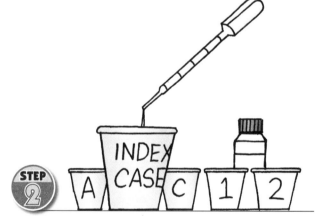

STEP 2

Add two capfuls of sodium hydroxide to the **Index Case**. **Swirl** to mix. Now **fill** a pipette with the Index Case solution. **Squirt** half into Cup A; half into Cup B. Next **fill** the pipette with Cup A solution. **Squirt** half into Cup 1; half into Cup 2.

STEP 3

Fill a pipette with Cup B solution. **Squirt** half into Cup 3; half into Cup 4. Now **pour** a little of the liquid in Cup C into Cup 5. (*Do not use the pipette for this!*) Carefully **record** each step thus far.

STEP 4

Using a clean pipette, **add** a few drops of phenolphthalein to each cup. **Record** the results in your journal. **Share** and **compare** observations with other research teams.

WHAT HAPPENED?

You just **modeled** how **disease** can spread rapidly beginning with just one person! Scientists call the rapid spread of a disease an **epidemic**. In this activity, the sodium hydroxide represented a disease. The **index case** cup represented the first person in an area to **contract** the disease. Notice this person only came into contact with two people (Cup A and Cup B). Then those two people came into contact with other groups (represented by Cups 1 though 4). The result? Several people got the disease very rapidly!

The **phenolphthalein** we used is a **chemical indicator** which changes color when it contacts a **base** (like sodium hydroxide). In this activity, it represents a medical testing procedure given to a person suspected of having a disease. Diseases that spread rapidly may be referred to as **contagious**, **infectious**, or **communicable**.

WHAT WE LEARNED

1 What do the cups in this activity represent?
Explain what the term "index case" means.

_____

_____

_____

_____

_____

_____

2 What does the sodium hydroxide represent?
Define the term "epidemic."

_____

_____

_____

_____

_____

_____

3 In Step 4, why did some cups show color and others didn't?
What did this represent?

_____

_____

_____

_____

_____

4 What does the phenolphthalein represent?
Why are medical tests important in an epidemic?

_____

_____

_____

_____

_____

5 Based on what you've learned, how do contagious diseases spread?
What steps might health authorities take to stop an epidemic?

_____

_____

_____

_____

_____

_____

CONCLUSION

Certain kinds of diseases can spread rapidly. The rapid spread of a contagious disease is called an epidemic. Such diseases are often spread through human contact.

FOOD FOR THOUGHT

2 Corinthians 7:1 Disease has been one of mankind's greatest enemies since earliest recorded history. Scripture contains many stories of how Jesus healed people who were very sick. Struggling to survive a disease is not a pleasant experience!

In this Scripture, Paul reminds us that our bodies are not the only thing that can experience sickness. Like a contagious disease, bad habits, wicked companions, or poor attitudes can infect our souls with the poison of sin. But staying close to Jesus can help us keep our hearts and minds disease free!

JOURNAL   My Science Notes

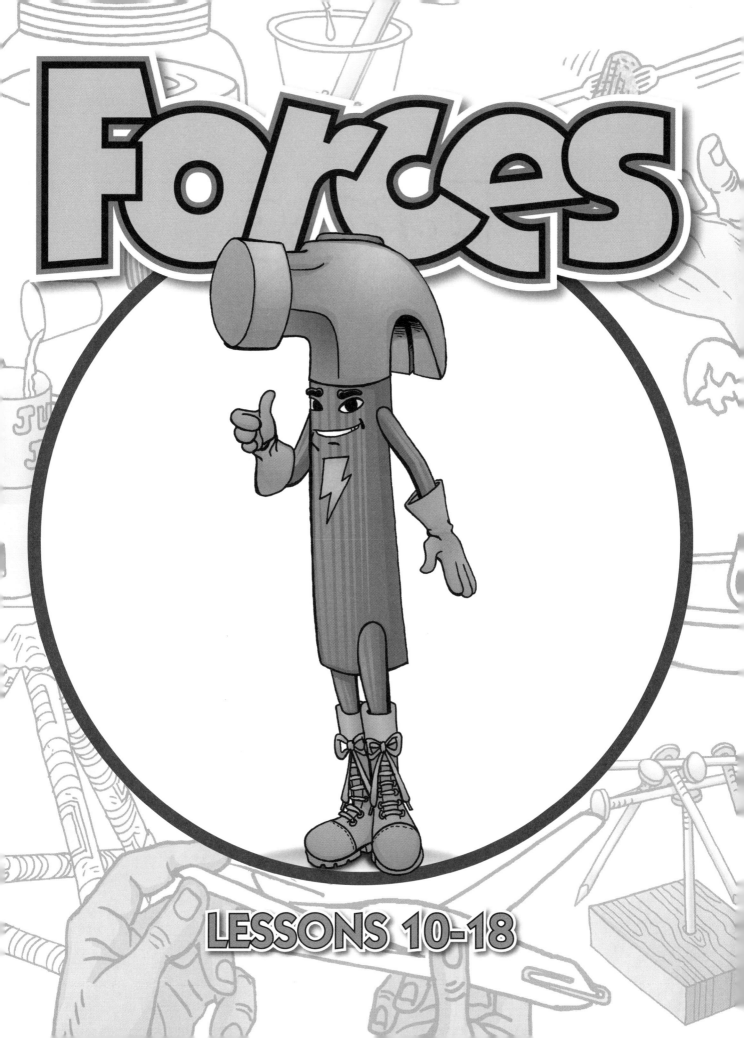

Forces

LESSONS 10-18

Forces

In this section, you'll discover how "**push** and **pull**" form the basis for all physical movement. You'll explore simple machines (levers, pulleys). You'll work with Newton's laws of motion. You'll even learn to understand concepts like torque, inertia, and buoyancy.

MAGNET MOTIONS

FOCUS   Magnetism

OBJECTIVE   To explore magnetic fields

OVERVIEW   Magnetism is a basic force that has fascinated mankind for centuries. In this activity, we'll explore some characteristics of a magnet.

WHAT TO DO

STEP 1

Touch the magnet to each of the following: wooden dowel, aluminum foil, pencil, paper, nail, paperclip, plastic. **Record** the results.

STEP 2

Two surfaces of the magnets will attract, the other two will repel. **Demonstrate** this by holding the magnets next to each other. **Record** the results, then flip one magnet over. **Record** the resulting change.

STEP 3

Slide a magnet over the end of a pencil. Now **slip** on a second magnet. (Don't let them slam together or they'll break!) **Record** the results. **Remove** the second magnet, flip it over, and **repeat**. **Record** the results.

STEP 4

Review each step in this activity. **Make notes** about what you discovered. **Share** and **compare** observations with your research team.

WHAT HAPPENED?

Some materials (like nails) attract **magnets**. Other materials (like aluminum foil) do not. **Metals** that attract magnets are called **ferrous** or **ferromagnetic**. They usually contain iron, nickel, or cobalt. Magnets can be **permanent** (like the ones we used), or **temporary**. Temporary magnets are made by wrapping **insulated** wire around ferromagnetic metal, then passing **direct current** (DC) **electricity** through the wire. When the current turns off, so does the magnet!

Magnets have opposite **poles** or ends called north and south. If you bring *unlike* poles (one north, one south) together, they **attract** each other. If you bring *like* poles (both north or both south) together, they **repel** each other. **Magnetic forces** help create **electricity**, drive electric motors, store data — or even perform simple tasks like holding messages on your refrigerator!

WHAT WE LEARNED

1 Which materials in Step 1 were ferromagnetic? Which materials were not? What are some common ingredients of ferromagnetic metals?

_____

_____

_____

_____

_____

_____

_____

2 Compare Step 2 and Step 3. How were they similar? How were they different? What characteristics of magnets did you discover?

_____

_____

_____

_____

_____

_____

_____

3 Explain the difference between "like" and "unlike" poles. Describe their behavior.

_____

_____

_____

_____

_____

_____

_____

4 Describe how temporary magnets are made. Why might a magnet like this be useful?

_____

_____

_____

_____

_____

_____

_____

5 Based on what you've learned, why wouldn't you stick notes to your computer with a refrigerator magnet?

_____

_____

_____

_____

_____

_____

_____

CONCLUSION

Some materials attract magnets, other materials do not. Magnets can be permanent or temporary. Like poles on a magnet repel each other, unlike poles attract.

FOOD FOR THOUGHT

John 15:17-19 Magnets repel or attract each other depending on how they're aligned. When magnets are not in the correct alignment, they won't stick together — no matter how hard you push them together!

This Scripture reminds us that God's children must stick together. Unbelievers often cause trouble for those who love God. In some countries, believers are persecuted or even killed. Yet Christians often create their own troubles by fighting among themselves! Why not ask God to align your heart so you're repelled by evil and attracted to good?

JOURNAL   My Science Notes

_____

_____

_____

_____

_____

_____

_____

_____

_____

_____

_____

_____

_____

_____

_____

_____

_____

_____

_____

_____

_____

PEANUT PASTE

FOCUS Adhesives

OBJECTIVE To explore how adhesives are tested for strength

OVERVIEW Adhesives hold things together. But some adhesives are stronger than others. In this activity, we'll model a test of adhesive strength.

WHAT TO DO

STEP 1

Drop four packing peanuts in a paper cup. **Add** water and **stir** with a craft stick to make a paste. (Use only enough water to make a good paste. Add water with the pipette so that you can accurately **count** and **record** the number of drops used.)

STEP 2

Cut a 1" x 8 1/2" strip of paper. **Draw** a line 1 inch from each end. **Coat** both 1 inch squares with a layer of paste, then **attach** this "handle" to a paper cup (see illustration) to make a tiny bucket. **Repeat** to make two more buckets. Let your buckets **dry** overnight.

STEP 3

[next day] **Lift** the "handle" of one bucket with a finger. **Hold** the bucket while a partner gently adds weights one at a time. When the handle breaks, **record** how many weights were used. **Repeat** with the other buckets.

STEP 4

Add the total number of weights and **divide** by three to find the average weight your glue held. **Make notes** about your adhesive recipe. **Share** and **compare** observations with other research teams.

WHAT HAPPENED?

You began this activity by making an **adhesive**. There are many kinds of adhesives designed for specific applications. But all adhesives have one thing in common: they hold things together! The simple adhesive you created was a thick **starch solution**, or paste, designed to hold two pieces of paper together.

The careful **measuring** and **recording** that you did **models** how scientists conduct **experiments**. Everything tested is the same except one thing (called the **variable**). You used the same number of packing peanuts, the same kind of paper, the same amount of paste. The only variable was the amount of water each team used. By comparing notes with other teams, you were able to determine the ideal (**optimum**) water content needed in the recipe to create the strongest paste.

WHAT WE LEARNED

1 Name at least three kinds of adhesives. What do all adhesives have in common? Why are there different kinds of adhesives?

_____

_____

_____

_____

_____

_____

_____

2 Describe the paste you created in step 2. Why was it important to let this paste dry overnight?

_____

_____

_____

_____

_____

_____

_____

3 Why were multiple "buckets" used in this activity? How did this add to the accuracy of the results? Why not just use one bucket for testing?

_____

_____

_____

_____

_____

_____

4 How much water did your team use in Step 1? How did this compare to other teams? Based on other teams' results, what is the optimum water content for this particular formula?

_____

_____

_____

_____

_____

_____

5 Describe the use of a variable in scientific testing. How does changing only one variable each time make testing more accurate?

_____

_____

_____

_____

_____

_____

CONCLUSION

Scientists conduct experiments to find answers. Scientific experiments must be carefully controlled, observed, and recorded to yield accurate results. Only one variable should be changed for each experiment.

FOOD FOR THOUGHT

Proverbs 18:24 The strength of a good adhesive can be surprising. If you have the right recipe, the bond can be even stronger than the surrounding materials! A good adhesive has the ability to hold things together no matter what happens.

Scripture reminds us the world is full of people who pretend to be friends until times get tough. Suddenly when you need them most, they're gone! But true friends are like an excellent adhesive. They'll stick with you even on those bad days. Remember, Jesus is the truest friend of all. No matter what happens, he'll always be there!

JOURNAL   My Science Notes

NAME _____

BALANCING NAILS

FOCUS Center of Gravity

OBJECTIVE To explore how objects balance

OVERVIEW Logical science principles can help us perform seemingly impossible tasks. In this activity, we'll use an object's center of gravity to balance six nails on one!

WHAT TO DO

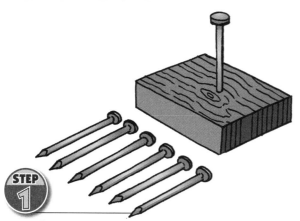

STEP 1

Place the wood block on your work surface with the nail sticking straight up. **Lay** six nails beside it. With your research team, **discuss** ways you might balance these nails on top of the nail in the block. **Make notes** and drawings.

STEP 2

Try the plan you devised in Step 1. If it doesn't work (and many won't), **devise** another plan, or **modify** the first plan and try again. **Record** the results in your journal.

STEP 3

[next day] **Listen** as your teacher explains one solution to the nail balancing problem. Now **try** to implement the solution. Once the nails are balanced, lightly **tap** the stack to see if it can maintain its balance. **Record** the results.

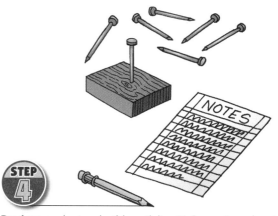

STEP 4

Review each step in this activity. **Make notes** about what happened and why. **Share** and **compare** observations with your research team.

WHAT HAPPENED?

To balance all those nails, you had to find the **balance point** (also called the **center of gravity**). The nails had to be arranged around this point so that there was an even **force** going in every direction. This balancing of forces is called **equilibrium**.

The center of gravity on a ruler is exactly in the middle. This is because its shape and **weight** are uniform. But don't be fooled! An object's center of gravity is based on the mid-point of its **mass**, not its shape.

Objects with odd shapes (like baseball bats), or objects with uniform shapes but unevenly distributed weight (like pencils with heavy erasers), have centers of gravity that are . . . off center! You'll find the mid-point of their mass toward the heavier end rather than at the center.

WHAT WE LEARNED

1 Describe your team's first attempt to balance the nails in Step 2. What was the result? Describe modifications to your first plan. What were the results?

_____

_____

_____

_____

_____

_____

_____

2 What is the scientific name for an object's "balance point"? What is a balancing of forces called?

_____

_____

_____

_____

_____

_____

_____

3 Describe the solution to the nail-balancing problem. Why did this solution work?

_____

_____

_____

_____

_____

_____

4 This activity is difficult, even when you know the solution! Explain how your "failures" helped you move toward a solution. How does this relate to the work scientists do?

_____

_____

_____

_____

_____

_____

5 Based on what you've learned, would the balance point of a hammer be near the handle end or the head? Explain your answer.

_____

_____

_____

_____

_____

_____

_____

CONCLUSION

All objects have a center of gravity. This "balance point" is based on the distribution of an object's mass, not just its shape.

FOOD FOR THOUGHT

1 Corinthians 3:10-12 This activity was tough to do, even when you knew the solution. Imagine how much harder it would have been if the support nail were loose! No matter how good you were at balancing, without a good foundation, your work would have collapsed.

In this Scripture, Paul reminds us that faith is much the same. Regardless of your ability, your education, or your wealth, if you don't build on a solid foundation, your work will be meaningless. But when you base your life on a relationship with Jesus and learn to trust in God's plans, you're building for eternity!

JOURNAL   My Science Notes

_____

_____

_____

_____

_____

_____

_____

_____

_____

_____

_____

_____

_____

_____

_____

_____

_____

_____

_____

NAME _____

CORKS & FORKS

FOCUS Torque and Equilibrium

OBJECTIVE To explore how forces can balance

OVERVIEW In our last lesson, we learned how to find an object's center of gravity. In this activity, we'll take a closer look at torque and equilibrium by building a "balanced" model.

WHAT TO DO

STEP 1

Insert the push pin in the exact middle of the large end of the cork. Now **place** the end of the pin on your finger tip and try to **balance** the cork. **Record** the results.

STEP 2

Push a fork into the cork. (Be gentle. They break easily!) Try to **balance** the cork again. **Record** the results using notes and drawings. Now **add** a second fork and try again. **Record** the results.

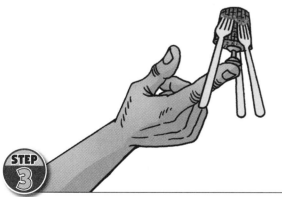

STEP 3

Add a third fork. **Rearrange** the forks until you can easily balance the cork. (Hint: Think of a tightrope walker!) Now gently **tap** one of the forks. **Record** the results. Make sure everyone on your team has a turn.

STEP 4

Review each step in this activity. **Make notes** about what did and did not work and why. **Share** and **compare** your observations with the other research teams.

As we learned in our last lesson, balancing **forces** is called **equilibrium**. Like children playing on a teeter-totter, the **weight** must be shifted until the forces are equal around the **center of gravity**.

There was another force involved in Step 4. When you tapped on one fork, the balanced arrangement tried to twist. This twisting movement is called **torque**.

You use torque every time you swing a bat, use a hammer, or perform any action that requires a circular or semi-circular motion. The arrangement handled the torque force well since movement of one fork was offset by the other fork. In other words, the cork's forks torque was balanced. (Try to say that one fast!)

WHAT WE LEARNED

1 Describe your attempts to balance the cork in Step 1. Why was it difficult?

_____

_____

_____

_____

_____

_____

_____

2 Describe how adding the forks in Step 2 helped or hurt your balancing efforts. Explain why this occurred.

_____

_____

_____

_____

_____

_____

_____

3 What difference did rearranging the forks (Step 3) make? What is this balancing of forces called?

_____

_____

_____

_____

_____

_____

4 What additional force was introduced in Step 4? What kind of force is this? What effect did it have on the balanced arrangement? Why?

_____

_____

_____

_____

_____

_____

5 Based on what you've learned, why do tight-rope walkers use long poles? Explain the forces involved and how the pole helps.

_____

_____

_____

_____

_____

_____

CONCLUSION

Forces can be balanced. Balanced forces are called equilibrium. Equilibrium can be achieved with many kinds of forces including torque (a twisting force).

FOOD FOR THOUGHT

Job 38:4-11 The purpose of science is to discover answers about the world around us. Deciding how to achieve equilibrium was a little tough, but with some time you figured it out. Scientists have figured out many useful things, leading to the inventions of new tools, new medicines, and new ways of doing things.

Sometimes people act like they have all the answers. But good scientists know that the more we learn, the more we discover new areas we know nothing about! This Scripture reminds us that God's knowledge, wisdom, and power are infinitely beyond our comprehension. Always remember that we serve an awesome God who created all the marvels of the Universe!

JOURNAL My Science Notes

_____

_____

_____

_____

_____

_____

_____

_____

_____

_____

_____

_____

_____

_____

_____

_____

_____

_____

_____

EGG AIRBAG

FOCUS Kinetic Energy

OBJECTIVE To explore how forces affect objects

OVERVIEW Many safety devices are based on understanding kinetic (moving) energy. In this activity, we'll explore how forces interact by creating a model.

WHAT TO DO

STEP 1

Decide how far you want to drop the egg. (Use this same distance if you need to repeat Step 2.) Now open the plastic bag and fluff it to get some air inside. Seal the bag tightly.

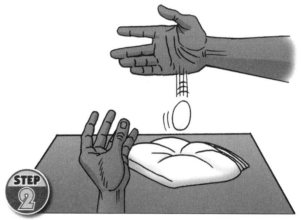

STEP 2

Place the bag in the middle of your work surface. Drop the egg onto the bag. (Ask team members to catch the egg if it bounces off!) Record the results.

STEP 3

If your egg broke, adjust the airbag and try again! If your egg didn't break, verify your bag's efficiency with a second drop. Now open your egg into a bowl and examine the yolk. Make notes about what you see.

STEP 4

Review the steps in this activity. Make notes on how distance and airbag firmness affected the results. Share and compare your observations with other research teams.

WHAT HAPPENED?

When you lifted the egg, you gave it **potential energy** (energy that's not moving). When you dropped the egg, you **converted** the potential energy into **kinetic energy** (energy that moves). **Gravity** was the **force** involved in both **storing** and **releasing** this energy.

Your bag used a principle similar to a car's airbag. The idea is to minimize damage to a moving object. The falling egg **pushes** on the air in the bag. The air in the bag pushes right back. Control comes from adjusting the force of the air. Too much air and the bag is too hard, cracking the egg's shell. Too little air and the bag is too limp, allowing the egg to hit the floor. The correct amount of air provides just the right amount of **opposing force**, cushioning the egg's fall to minimize damage.

WHAT WE LEARNED

1 How far did you drop the egg in Step 1? How would increasing or decreasing this distance affect the results?

_____

_____

_____

_____

_____

_____

_____

2 Why must the bag be tightly sealed in Step 2? How might a poorly sealed bag affect the results?

_____

_____

_____

_____

_____

_____

_____

3 Compare the yolk of your egg (Step 3) with the yolk of other teams' eggs. How were they similar? How were they different? What caused these differences?

_____

_____

_____

_____

_____

_____

4 Name two kinds of energy involved in this activity. How are they similar? How are they different?

_____

_____

_____

_____

_____

_____

5 Based on what you've learned, how does a car's airbag protect you in an accident? List potential problems airbag designers might face.

_____

_____

_____

_____

_____

_____

CONCLUSION

Potential energy is non-moving energy. Kinetic energy is moving energy. Moving energy contains force which can cause injury unless an appropriate opposing force is applied.

FOOD FOR THOUGHT

Romans 8:38-39 Thanks to an appropriate use of opposing force, your egg suffered only minimal damage. It was rushing downward toward certain destruction when the airbag intervened. It saved your egg from serious harm.

This Scripture talks about a similar kind of protection. Paul reminds us that nothing in Heaven or Earth can separate us from God's endless love. Even in those times when we're willfully rushing toward certain destruction, God is always listening for our call for help. His power can provide the opposing force that counteracts the evil actions of Satan, protecting our souls from a disastrous crash.

JOURNAL My Science Notes

_____

_____

_____

_____

_____

_____

_____

_____

_____

_____

_____

_____

_____

_____

_____

_____

_____

_____

_____

_____

NAME _____

BUOYANT BALL

FOCUS Buoyancy

OBJECTIVE To explore why some objects float

OVERVIEW Punch a hole in an air mattress, and it sinks. Punch a hole in a life-preserver and it still floats! What's the difference? In this activity, we'll explore how buoyancy works.

WHAT TO DO

STEP 1

Fill the clear jar with water to within 1/2 inch of the top. Gently **drop** a washer into the jar. **Record** the results. **Remove** the washer and **refill** the jar if necessary.

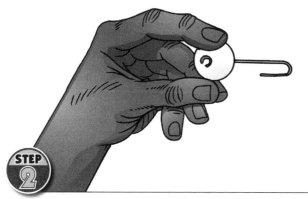

STEP 2

Drop the small styrofoam® ball in the water. **Record** the results. **Remove** the ball and **poke** the wire through it. **Bend** one end down against the ball. **Bend** the other end into a fish hook shape.

STEP 3

Hang a washer on the end of the wire. **Place** the ball in the water. **Record** the results. **Add** washers one at a time until the top of the ball is at the water's surface. **Record** the total number of washers used.

STEP 4

Repeat Steps 2 and 3 with the larger ball. **Record** the results. Now **review** each step in this activity and **make notes** about what you discovered. **Share** and **compare** observations with your research team.

WHAT HAPPENED?

All **matter** on Earth is constantly being **pulled** downward by **gravity**. To keep an object from sinking, gravity has to be overcome (**pushed**) by another force. The **opposing force** pushing in this activity is called **buoyancy**.

An object's buoyancy primarily depends on its **density**. Steel is very dense, so it sinks. But steel boats float because their shape **displaces** water with air. The air is less dense than water, so the boat floats (unless a hole lets water in!). Like many life preservers, the ball in this activity is made of Styrofoam® — a material that's full of trapped air. Unlike an air mattress, punching a hole in Styrofoam® doesn't let the air out. In fact, if you grind Styrofoam® into small pieces (not recommended), every tiny piece will still float because it's still full of air!

WHAT WE LEARNED

1 **Describe what happened to the washer in Step 1. Why did this happen?**

_____

_____

_____

_____

_____

_____

_____

2 **Describe what happened to the styrofoam ball in Step 2? Why did this happen?**

_____

_____

_____

_____

_____

_____

_____

3 How did adding washers change the ball's buoyancy in Step 3? Compare this with the behavior of the larger ball in Step 4.

_____

_____

_____

_____

_____

_____

4 Buoyancy depends primarily on what characteristic? Explain why steel ships float.

_____

_____

_____

_____

_____

_____

_____

5 Based on what you've learned, could a life preserver be made from steel? Why or why not?

_____

_____

_____

_____

_____

_____

_____

CONCLUSION

Buoyancy is a force that opposes gravity. An object's buoyancy depends primarily on its density. Buoyancy can also be seen as the amount of liquid an object can displace.

FOOD FOR THOUGHT

Isaiah 41:10 The Styrofoam® ball in this activity held up a lot of weight. Its buoyancy was able to overcome the force of gravity that was pulling the washers down. In fact, it held up a great deal compared to what it weighed!

In a way, this activity represents the continual battle between good and evil. God holds us up while evil constantly tries to drag us down. This Scripture reminds us that God's power and love conquer all. He promises to strengthen us and hold us up in his arms of love. In the truest sense, God is our ultimate life preserver!

JOURNAL My Science Notes

_____

_____

_____

_____

_____

_____

_____

_____

_____

_____

_____

_____

_____

_____

_____

_____

_____

_____

_____

_____

PAPER PYRAMID

FOCUS Transfer of Forces

OBJECTIVE To explore how structure affects strength

OVERVIEW Does strength come only from materials used, or does how they're put together (structure) play a role? In this activity, we'll explore the answer using a sheet of newspaper.

WHAT TO DO

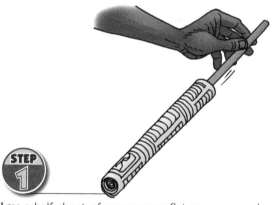

STEP 1

Lay a half sheet of newspaper flat on your work surface. **Place** a straw at the top and **roll** the paper tightly around it. **Remove** the straw once you're done, but keep the roll tight. **Finish** by taping the roll securely.

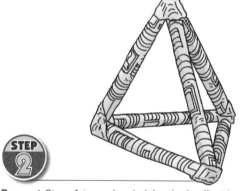

STEP 2

Repeat Step 1 to make six identical rolls. Now **tape** three rolls together to make a triangle. **Place** this flat on your work surface, then **attach** a roll at each corner. **Tape** the ends of these together to make a three-sided pyramid.

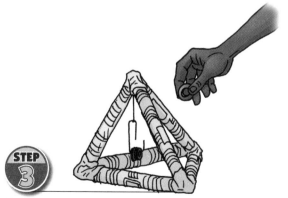

STEP 3

Check your corners to make sure they're securely taped. **Attach** a bent paperclip to the top point with string (see illustration). **Test** your **Paper Pyramid** by hanging weights on the paperclip. Slowly **add** more weights until you run out or your pyramid collapses.

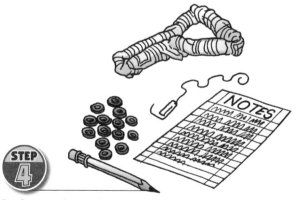

STEP 4

Review each step in this activity. **Compare** the strength of six paper sheets to the six paper rolls you made. **Share** and **compare** observations about your pyramid with the other research teams.

WHAT HAPPENED?

Most paper is made from **wood fibers**. Trees are strong because the wood fibers are all connected together. When wood is ground up and treated with chemicals to make paper, the fibers are separated and smoothed into sheets. This helps make paper easy to write on, read, and fold. (Imagine doing this with a piece of bark!)

One sheet of newspaper is pretty flimsy. But when you roll it up, you're putting **layers** of separated wood fibers back together again. Then when you attach rolls together, you create a **structure** that has a lot of strength!

As you saw, **force** (weight) is easily **transferred** through the rolls by the design of the structure. Transferring force allows all parts of the structure to share the **load**.

WHAT WE LEARNED

1 Compare a sheet of newspaper with the newspaper roll you made in Step 1. How were they similar? How were they different?

_____

_____

_____

_____

_____

_____

_____

2 Compare one newspaper roll with the pyramid you made in Step 2. How were they similar? How were they different?

_____

_____

_____

_____

_____

_____

_____

3 When your pyramid finally collapsed, what was its weakest point? How could you have made this stronger?

_____

_____

_____

_____

_____

_____

4 What geometric shape is a pyramid made from? Compare the pyramid's ability to support weight to that of a cube. Which is stronger? Why?

_____

_____

_____

_____

_____

_____

5 Based on what you've learned, why are diagonal braces used at the corners of fences?

_____

_____

_____

_____

_____

_____

_____

CONCLUSION

Materials are usually stronger in layers. Layered materials can help transfer forces from one part of a structure to another one.

FOOD FOR THOUGHT

1 Thessalonians 5:11 The flimsy sheet of newspaper couldn't hold very much on its own. But when you rolled it into a tight cylinder, it gained a lot of strength. Then when you attached it to other cylinders, it became part of a strong, unified structure.

On our own we can't do much. In our weakness, it's easy to fail. Yet when we wrap ourselves in God's love, we gain needed strength. This Scripture reminds us of another important step. We must learn to encourage and support one another in Christian love. When God's children begin to work together, they become part of a strong, unified "structure" that helps spread God's goodness throughout the world.

JOURNAL My Science Notes

_____

_____

_____

_____

_____

_____

_____

_____

_____

_____

_____

_____

_____

_____

_____

_____

_____

_____

_____

PAPER PILLAR

FOCUS Transfer of Forces

OBJECTIVE To explore how shape relates to strength

OVERVIEW Combining materials correctly (structure) can help transfer forces. But can a material's shape affect its ability to transfer force as well? In this activity, we'll build a model to find out!

WHAT TO DO

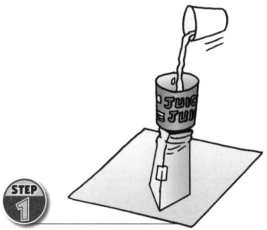

STEP 1

How much water will a piece of paper hold up? Working with your research team, **fold** or **bend** a sheet of paper to hold up a juice can. Now slowly **fill** the can with water until the paper collapses. **Record** the results.

STEP 2

Let's try again! **Lay** a dry sheet of paper on your work surface, long side facing you. **Mark** down the paper's right side at 1", 2", and 3". Do the same down the left side. Now **draw** lines across the paper connecting each set of marks.

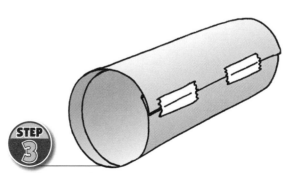

STEP 3

Fold the paper flat along the first line. **Fold** it over again at the second and third lines. Now **roll** the paper into a tube and tuck one end about 1" inside the flap. **Tape** the seam securely. (The paper must stay dry at all times!)

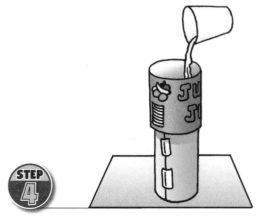

STEP 4

Use your "paper pillar" to **repeat** Step 1. **Record** the results and **make notes** about similarities and differences to Step 1. **Share** and **compare** your observations with other research teams.

WHAT HAPPENED?

Generally the more **material** you use the stronger the **structure**. But there's a problem! More material creates greater **weight** and also drives up costs. Not enough material, however, makes for a weak and possibly unsafe structure. That's why engineers try to design structures with materials and **shapes** that offer great strength, but are also lighter and less expensive.

That was the focus of this activity. Although it used the same amount of material, the reinforced tube you created was a much stronger shape. This different shape allowed the paper's **molecules** to work together in a more efficient fashion. More efficient shapes help **transfer** the **forces**. In this case, the weight of the water was transferred to your work surface, which transferred the weight to the floor, which transferred the weight to the ground.

WHAT WE LEARNED

1 **Describe what happened in Step 1.**
How much water (weight) did your first structure hold?

_____

_____

_____

_____

_____

_____

_____

2 **What was the purpose of the folds in Step 2?**
What effect did the folds have on the paper's molecules?

_____

_____

_____

_____

_____

_____

_____

3 Why did the seams have to be taped securely? What might have happened if the tape's adhesive was weak? Why?

_____

_____

_____

_____

_____

_____

4 Describe a building component that's similar to the Paper Pillar you created. What does this component support? Why is this support important?

_____

_____

_____

_____

_____

_____

5 Based on what you've learned, how does shape help transfer force? Give at least three common examples of a column or pillar shape transferring force.

_____

_____

_____

_____

_____

_____

CONCLUSION

The shape of a material can affect its strength, helping it to more efficiently transfer force.

FOOD FOR THOUGHT

Psalms 18:16-18 It didn't seem like a simple sheet of paper could hold up even an empty can, let alone the weight of all that water. But once everything was in the right relationship, it worked! The paper was able to hold up an amazing amount of water.

This Scripture reminds us that God often accomplishes seemingly impossible tasks. When we're drowning in troubles, when we're surrounded by those who would do us harm, when we're at our very weakest — God steps in and lifts us up in his loving arms. Always remember, when you're in a right relationship with God, amazing things can happen!

JOURNAL My Science Notes

_____

_____

_____

_____

_____

_____

_____

_____

_____

_____

_____

_____

_____

_____

_____

_____

_____

_____

LESSON 18

FOAM FLYER

FOCUS Flight

OBJECTIVE To explore factors that affect flight

OVERVIEW What makes something fly? Can you make a glider from a flat piece of Styrofoam®? In this activity, we'll explore flight by making a model.

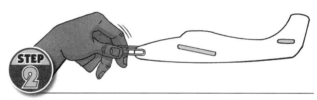

WHAT TO DO

STEP 1

Remove the "Foam Flyer" page from the back of your worktext. **Cut out** the pattern parts and **lay** them on the Styrofoam® tray. **Trace** around all three parts, then carefully **cut** them out. **Smooth** any rough edges with sandpaper.

STEP 2

Cut the slots for the elevator and wing. (If the Styrofoam® breaks, repair it with tape.) **Slip** the elevator and wing through the slots, then **push** a paperclip onto the nose. **Decorate** your team's flyer as desired.

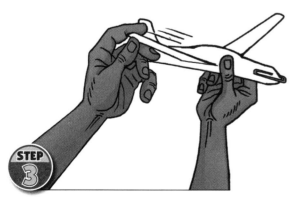

STEP 3

Begin test flights. After each flight, **modify** or **adjust** the wings, elevator, or paperclip. (Your teacher will have suggestions.) Be sure to **change** only one thing (variable) for each flight! **Record** the results.

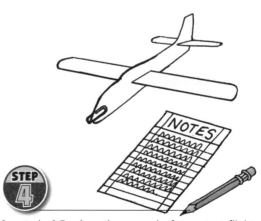

STEP 4

[next day] **Review** the record of your test flights. **Discuss** what changes were made and the effect they had on the flyer's performance. **Share** and **compare** observations with other research teams.

WHAT HAPPENED?

Flight is possible because fast-moving air has lower **air pressure**. This is called the **Bernoulli Principle** (named after the man who discovered this). Because of a wing's **shape** (or angle), air moves faster over the top than it does under the bottom, creating **low air pressure** on top of the wing. This causes the **higher air pressure** under the wing to **push** up. The result is known as **lift**.

So why don't sitting planes just rise into the sky? Because air isn't moving fast enough to create the large air pressure differences needed for lift. Some kind of **force** must be applied. Usually the force is provided by a motor with a propeller or by a jet engine. This makes the plane move faster until air **speeds** are high enough to provide lift. In this activity, you provided the force by flinging your **Foam Flyer** toward the sky!

WHAT WE LEARNED

1 Why was it important to smooth the rough edges in Step 1? What effect could rough edges have on air flow?

_____

_____

_____

_____

_____

_____

_____

2 What characteristic of a wing creates lift on an airplane? Explain how this works.

_____

_____

_____

_____

_____

_____

_____

3 Describe the test flights in Step 3. What variables did you change? What effect did these changes have?

_____

_____

_____

_____

_____

_____

4 What is the name of the effect that fast-moving air has on air pressure? How is this important for flight?

_____

_____

_____

_____

_____

_____

5 Based on what you've learned, how are hawks, eagles, seagulls, and similar birds able to fly for long periods of time without flapping their wings? Explain your answer.

_____

_____

_____

_____

_____

_____

CONCLUSION

Fast-moving air creates lower air pressure. This is called the Bernoulli Principle. The curved surface of a wing uses this principle to create lift, which leads to flight.

FOOD FOR THOUGHT

2 Corinthians 5:17 Who would have thought you could turn a plain styrofoam® tray into something that could fly? With a little time and effort, you were able to create something brand-new!

In this Scripture, Paul reminds us that God can make *us* brand-new. The bad things in our past are forgiven, and we begin a clean, new life. Through the power of Jesus' love, our hearts are changed, and we begin to reach out to others in care and compassion. Remember that God can take anyone, no matter how plain or ordinary, and turn them into something special!

JOURNAL   My Science Notes

Earth

LESSONS 19-27

Earth Science

Earth Science is the study of **earth** and **sky**. In this section you'll explore the structure of our planet (rocks, crystals, volcanos), the atmosphere (air, clouds), and related systems (water cycles, air pressure, weather). Grades 7 and 8 reach out even further with a look at the solar system and stars.

NAME _____

OCEAN OF AIR

FOCUS Atmospheric Pressure

OBJECTIVE To explore the force of air pressure

OVERVIEW Everyone knows we're surrounded by an "ocean" of air. You may think of air as weightless. But is it? In this activity, we'll explore this idea by trying to break a toothpick with air!

WHAT TO DO

STEP 1

Lay a flat toothpick on your work surface so that about a third of it is sticking out over the edge. Make sure the area is clear, then try to **break** the toothpick by flipping the end with your index finger. **Record** the results.

STEP 2

Lay the toothpick back on your work surface and cover it with six sheets of newspaper. Make sure the papers are very flat and even with the edge. Now **push** down quickly, but gently, on the end of the toothpick. **Record** the results.

STEP 3

Repeat Step 2, but instead of pushing gently, **flip** the end with your index finger as in Step 1. **Hit** the end hard! **Record** the results.

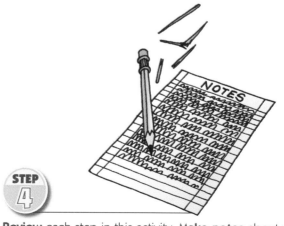

STEP 4

Review each step in this activity. **Make notes** about what you discovered. **Predict** how air pressure may have played a role in the results of Step 3. **Share** and **compare** observations with your research team.

WHAT HAPPENED?

In Step 1, the toothpick shot off the table. In Step 2, the toothpick raised the papers and fell off the table. But in Step 3, the toothpick broke! What happened? Obviously some kind of **force** was holding the toothpick back.

The force pushing down was **air pressure**. The large **surface area** of the newspaper **transferred** this pressure to surface of the toothpick. (Step 2 proved it wasn't just the newspaper's **weight**.) When you **pushed** the toothpick slowly, the **air molecules** had time to shift their weight aside. But when you moved rapidly, the toothpick pushed against the full pressure of the air. The resulting **resistance** (force) of the air broke the toothpick.

WHAT WE LEARNED

1 **In Step 1, why didn't the toothpick break?**
How much surface area was the air pressure pushing on?

2 **In Step 2, why didn't the toothpick break?**
How was the speed you pushed on the toothpick a factor?

3 In Step 3, why did the toothpick break?
How much surface area was the air pressure pushing on?

4 Explain how force was transferred in this activity.

5 Based on what you've learned, variations in what characteristic of air might affect weather? Why?

CONCLUSION

We're surrounded by an ocean of air. Its pressure is constantly pushing on us — but we don't notice because our bodies are pushing back with equal force.

FOOD FOR THOUGHT

James 1:5-8 At first, you may have doubted that air could break a toothpick. Certainly at first glance, it seemed impossible! But you trusted your teacher, followed the instructions, and SNAP! Mission accomplished.

Many times in life we have to act based on our faith. We have to trust God, follow his instructions, and know that the results are in his hands. This Scripture reminds us that God is always ready to help us, ready to lead in the plan of our lives. As our relationship with God deepens, we will learn to trust him more and more, no matter how impossible the situation seems.

JOURNAL   My Science Notes

CLASSIFIED CLOUDS

FOCUS   Weather

OBJECTIVE   To explore clouds' relationship to weather

OVERVIEW   Ever wonder about tomorrow's weather? Clouds are one way that meteorologists predict the weather. In this activity, we'll explore names and characteristics of clouds.

WHAT TO DO

STEP 1

When scientists study something, they need data (information). Today your teacher will tell you about the characteristics of clouds. This is the basic data for this activity, so **listen** carefully and **take** good **notes**!

STEP 2

[next day] **Remove** the **Classified Clouds** page from the back of your worktext. Working with your research team and using your notes from yesterday, **label** each picture according to the cloud's characteristics.

STEP 3

Add more labels as needed. If you can estimate a cloud's height, **add** the appropriate prefix. If you see indications of moisture, **add** an additional prefix or suffix. **Get input** from your team, but make your own decisions as you label your page.

STEP 4

Demonstrate your mastery of cloud terminology by drawing three more clouds in your journal. Be sure to **label** them appropriately. **Share** and **compare** observations (and drawings) with your research team.

WHAT HAPPENED?

Clouds are a visible form of water in the air. Although we usually think of clouds in a **gaseous** (water vapor) state, they can also be a **liquid** (suspended rain) or even a **solid** (tiny ice crystals). Most weather involves clouds and the various forms of moisture they carry.

The **Sun** provides the **energy** that creates **weather**. The amount of **solar energy** varies depending on the location and season. In northern **climates** or winter months, the low **heat energy** can cause moisture in the air to **freeze**, creating ice, snow, and sleet. In southern climates or summer months, high heat energy can cause moisture to **evaporate**.

These changes in **temperature** and moisture mix the **atmosphere's** energy, helping it **circulate** around the planet.

WHAT WE LEARNED

1 What three specific terms describe clouds based on their height? What does each term mean?

_____

_____

_____

_____

_____

_____

2 Which of the three "states of matter" apply to clouds? Give examples.

_____

_____

_____

_____

_____

_____

3 Compare stratonimbus and cumlonimbus clouds. How are they similar? How are they different?

_____

_____

_____

_____

_____

4 Based on what you've learned, describe the characteristics of an "altostratusnimbus" cloud.

_____

_____

_____

_____

_____

5 If changes in temperature and moisture didn't circulate around the Earth, what would countries around the equator be like? What would far northern countries be like?

_____

_____

_____

_____

_____

CONCLUSION

The sun provides the energy that produces weather. Weather changes are usually indicated by clouds. Weather changes help distribute moisture and atmospheric energy around the Earth.

FOOD FOR THOUGHT

Psalm 104:5-13 Clouds are wonderful indicators of the weather to come. This can be helpful when we're making plans for an afternoon picnic or a day at the lake. But weather forecasting isn't an exact science. Sometimes weather doesn't turn out to be what we'd hoped for!

When making plans for your life, wouldn't you prefer something more reliable than a weather forecast? This Scripture reminds us that God is the master planner! When the storms of life rage around you, God can keep you safe from harm. Why not let God take control of your life?

JOURNAL My Science Notes

MARVELOUS MAPPING

FOCUS   Remote Sensing

OBJECTIVE   To explore how inaccessible locations are mapped

OVERVIEW   There are undersea maps of places that no that human has ever been. How is this possible? In this activity, we'll explore the principle of how such maps are made.

WHAT TO DO

STEP 1

Cover the bottom of a shoebox with paper mache' paste. As it drys, **form** it to represent a stretch of deep unexplored ocean bottom. It may **include** plains, valleys, canyons, even undersea mountains! Let it dry overnight.

STEP 2

[next day] **Follow** your teacher's instructions to make a one-inch grid on the shoebox lid. **Label** the long lines A, B, C, etc. **Label** the short lines 1, 2, 3, etc. Carefully use a sharp pencil to **punch holes** at A1, A2, etc. **Tape** the lid on the box securely.

STEP 3

[next day] **Trade** boxes with another team. **Mark** a straw with 1/2 inch lines. **Explore** the "ocean bottom" by pushing the straw down hole A1. **Record** the depth. **Repeat** with holes A2, A3, etc. Now **transfer** the information to graph paper.

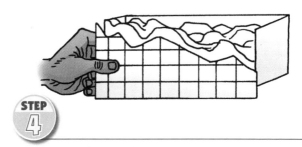

STEP 4

Connect the dots on the paper to create a cross-section, then **cut** away the top portion. Carefully **peel back** the side of the box and **place** the paper against the "ocean bottom" to see how they compare. **Share** observations with other research teams.

WHAT HAPPENED?

The method you used to make your map is called **remote sensing**. Using an **energy beam** (radar, sonar, laser, etc.) as a **probe**, scientists can measure distances between points very accurately. This **technology** was originally developed by NASA for the space program. Long-range probes help scientists collect information about places that humans may never go.

However, the map you made wasn't nearly as accurate as actually viewing the contour of your model's surface. This is because your **data points** (the places you took measurements) were relatively far apart. The more data points you sample, the better picture you get.

Even though they provide only an incomplete picture, remote sensing maps can help us gain a much better understanding of Earth's surface.

WHAT WE LEARNED

1 **Describe the surface you created in Step 1. What were its most notable features?**

_____

_____

_____

_____

_____

_____

2 **Explain how the letters and numbers added in Step 2 help identify a specific hole.**

_____

_____

_____

_____

_____

3 What was the purpose of the 1/2" lines on the straw?
Explain how they relate to the graph you produced in Step 4.

4 Compare the features of the surface you created in Step 1 with actual
surface features. Other than under the ocean, where might you find
similar contours on Earth?

5 How was your graph similar to the actual bottom contours? How was
it different? How could you have made it more accurate?

CONCLUSION

Remote sensing provides a way to map places humans can't go. Even though such maps provide less detail (inaccuracy of scale), they still help increase scientists' understanding of an area.

FOOD FOR THOUGHT

Genesis 1:9-10 Can you imagine what a huge job it would be to accurately sample the bottom of a large lake? Even data points a few yards apart could miss ledges and rock outcroppings. How much more difficult would it be to accurately map the world's oceans?

This Scripture reminds us God created both the oceans and dry land. He knows their every detail. It's the same way with our lives. At best, we can see only a limited number of life's data points, and sometimes it's hard to make good decisions. But when we trust God to direct our lives, we're guided by one who sees the whole picture!

JOURNAL   My Science Notes

NAME _____

COOKED COAL

FOCUS Earth Materials

OBJECTIVE To explore the properties of coal

OVERVIEW Heat a rock and you'll get . . . a hot rock. But not all "rocks" are the same. In this activity, we'll explore a rock-like material that's a major source of energy!

WHAT TO DO

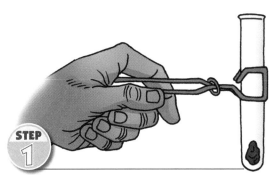

STEP 1

Observe the coal and describe it in your journal. Now **drop** the coal into the test tube and **place** the test tube into the test tube holder. **Predict** what might happen when the coal is heated.

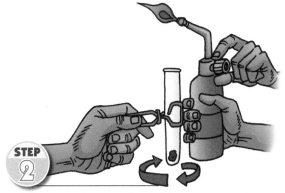

STEP 2

Carefully **hold** the test tube holder as your teacher heats the coal. (Make certain the opening of the tube is facing away from everyone.) **Watch** what happens inside the tube. **Record** the results, including any odors you notice.

STEP 3

Continue to **watch** as the coal begins to cool back down. (Remember, the tube is still HOT!) **Observe** the material left in the tube. **Make notes** about what you see. **Discard** the tube as indicated by your teacher.

STEP 4

Review each step in this activity. **Make notes** and drawings about what you observed. **Share** and **compare** observations with your research team.

WHAT HAPPENED?

Coal looks a lot like **rock** (or even dirt or dust), but it certainly reacts in a different way! When you "cook" coal, complicated things happen. The coal changes states from **solid** to **liquid** to **gas** back to a liquid. These are **physical** changes.

The coal also goes through a **chemical** change. As it's heated, it gives off **coal gas** and leaves behind **coal tar**. Coal gas was once a major source of **energy**, similar to natural gas or propane. People used it to light their homes and businesses. Coal tar is a complex stew of chemicals used in such diverse products as medicine and plastic!

As the coal cools, the residue it leaves behind is called **coke**. Coke is a very concentrated energy source used in the production of iron and steel.

WHAT WE LEARNED

1 Describe the coal in Step 1. How was it similar to the material left in Step 3? How was it different?

2 What did you predict in Step 1? How did this prediction reflect what actually happened?

3 Describe what happened in Step 2. What did the coal do as it was heated? Describe any odors you detected.

_____

_____

_____

_____

_____

_____

4 What "states of matter" occurred during this activity. Were these chemical or physical changes? Explain your answer.

_____

_____

_____

_____

_____

_____

5 Based on what you observed in Step 3, why is coal gas not an ideal residential energy source? What energy source do most American homes now use for light? How does this relate to coal?

_____

_____

_____

_____

_____

_____

_____

CONCLUSION

Properties of similar-looking earth materials can vary widely. Coal is an earth material used as an energy source. Coal is composed of useful and complicated chemicals that can be released by heating.

FOOD FOR THOUGHT

2 Corinthians 5:17 Some serious changes took place inside that test tube when heat was applied! The coal experienced both physical and chemical changes in its nature. These changes made the coal into several much more valuable substances.

Scripture tells us that major changes take place in our natures when God takes control of our hearts. As we get closer to God, we better reflect his love. Our selfish natures begin to be replaced with a spirit of compassion and caring. Although God may put us through the fires of trials and trouble, these obstacles only serve to make us more valuable in his service.

JOURNAL My Science Notes

NAME _____

SPACIOUS SPACE

FOCUS Solar System

OBJECTIVE To explore relative distances between planets

OVERVIEW The enormous distances of space are often hard to comprehend. In this activity, we'll explore relative distances between planets by making a scale model.

WHAT TO DO

STEP 1

Our solar system model will use a scale of one inch equals one million miles. Even so, it will require an entire football field! **Calculate** how long it would take to travel a million miles at 500 miles per hour. **Record** this in your journal.

STEP 2

Using an encyclopedia or the Internet, **list** the nine planets in order and tell how far each one is from the Sun. Using construction paper, **make** a large sign for the planet that the teacher assigns to your team.

STEP 3

A basketball on the goal line represents the Sun. Using the scale in Step 1, try to **calculate** where your planet should be and go to that spot. When the teacher calls out the correct locations, **move** as needed. **Record** any differences.

STEP 4

Note that at this scale, the Sun would actually be about the size of a marble, and the earth smaller than the head of a pin! Now **review** each step in this activity. **Share** and **compare** observations with your research team.

WHAT HAPPENED?

A group of **planets** that **orbit** (circle) a **star** is called a **solar system**. A group of solar systems (and other space bodies) that rotate around together are called a **galaxy**. The galaxy that contains our solar system is the **Milky Way**. Scientists estimate that the Milky Way contains over four hundred billion solar systems.

The **scale model** we made represents only the planets orbiting our **Sun**. The distance between other objects in the **universe** is almost unimaginable! For this activity, we used average distances since the paths planets follow are not really circles. Some orbits are so different that there are times Neptune is closer to the Sun than Pluto!

WHAT WE LEARNED

1 What two planets are Earth's closest neighbors? What is the relationship of these planets and Earth to the Sun?

2 In the scale we used, what distance does a foot represent? What distance does a yard represent? Traveling ten thousand miles per hour, about how far could you go in one day?

3 Why couldn't we show the planets in the correct scale on this model? Based on distance to the sun, which two planets would be the coldest? Which two planets would be the hottest?

4 What is a group of planets orbiting a star called? What is a group of solar systems rotating together called? What is the name of the galaxy that contains our solar system?

5 If you could fly through space at ten thousand miles per hour, how likely would you be to run into another planet? Explain your answer.

CONCLUSION

A group of planets orbiting a star is called a solar system. A group of solar systems rotating together is called a galaxy. The distance between a star and a planet determines the amount of energy it receives.

FOOD FOR THOUGHT

Psalm 89:11 It's hard to imagine a solar system without the sun. Imagine what would happen to the planets! They would be barren and cold, wandering aimlessly through space. The sun not only keeps the planets in their appointed orbits, but also provides the energy that allows for life.

Just as the sun is the center of the solar system, so God should be the center of our lives. His power is what keeps us headed in the right direction. His love provides the force that gives us life. Keep God at the center of your universe!

JOURNAL My Science Notes

NAME _____

PLANET PERSPECTIVE

FOCUS Solar System

OBJECTIVE To explore relative sizes of planets

OVERVIEW In Lesson 23, we explored relative distances between planets. In this activity, we'll explore the relative size of our solar system's planets.

WHAT TO DO

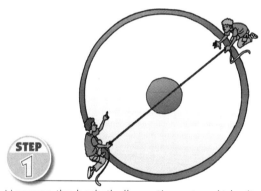

STEP 1

Measure the basketball court's center circle. It should be 12 feet across (a circle with a six-foot radius). This circle will represent the sun. **Pick** a planet and **estimate** how big it might be compared to this sun. **Record** your prediction

STEP 2

With a 12 foot sun, the scale is one inch equals 6,000 miles. **Calculate** the exact size to scale for any planet the teacher assigns your team. (Hint: Divide the planet's diameter by 6,000.)

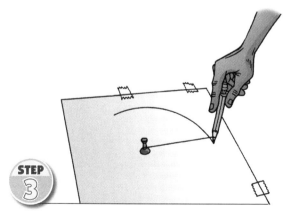

STEP 3

Make a one-dimensional (flat) model of your planet. Use a compass or string/pencil to **draw** the circles. If your planet is too small to label, **make** a small sign to go with it. **Take turns** placing your planets around the sun.

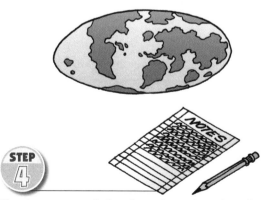

STEP 4

Check your prediction from Step 1 against the correct model. Now **review** each step in this activity. **Make notes** and drawings about what you observed. **Share** and **compare** observations with your research team.

WHAT HAPPENED?

Since **planets** are too large to fit in the gym, we used a **scale model** to compare relative sizes. (If you've ever made a model airplane or model car, you understand the concept of scale models.) Scientists and engineers make models all the time to teach, to test ideas, and to enhance their understanding of an object or idea.

In this model, it was obvious that the planets varied enormously in size! But in addition to size, planets can vary in **composition**, **temperature**, **atmosphere**, and other major ways. For instance, Venus is similar in size to Earth, but the average surface temperature is 900 degrees Fahrenheit, and the atmosphere is filled with clouds of sulfuric acid. Not a place designed to support life as we know it!

WHAT WE LEARNED

1 **What did you predict in Step 1? How did this prediction reflect the correct answer?**

2 **America is about 3,000 miles across. In the scale you used for this activity, about how far would that be?**

3 In your model, what two planets were the smallest? What two planets were the biggest? How does this compare to the real planets in our solar system? Why?

_____

_____

_____

_____

_____

4 "Planets of the same size are similar in most ways." Is this statement true or false? Explain your answer.

_____

_____

_____

_____

_____

5 How does the size of the moon compare to that of Earth? How does it compare to the Sun? Why does the Moon look about the same size as the Sun when viewed from Earth?

_____

_____

_____

_____

? CONCLUSION

Planets vary significantly in size as well as other characteristics. Scale models help scientists to study relationships between objects.

FOOD FOR THOUGHT

Matthew 10:29 The scale model you made helped you visualize the relative sizes of the planets in our solar system. It's amazing how insignificant the Earth looks in comparison to the Sun. A human being on this scale would be much smaller than the tiniest grain of sand!

Yet even though we're very small in comparison to the mighty, marvelous things God has made, God still knows each one of us individually. This Scripture tells us that God even notices the fall of a tiny bird. Next time you look at the night sky and contemplate the immensity of the stars, remember that God's love for you is as infinite as the universe.

JOURNAL My Science Notes

NAME _____

STAR STRUCTURES

FOCUS Constellations

OBJECTIVE To explore the star patterns seen from Earth

OVERVIEW The night sky is a jumble of stars — but if you look closely, some groups of stars seem to form patterns. In this activity, we'll explore some star patterns that have names!

WHAT TO DO

STEP 1

Help your team members **glue** black paper on a large piece of foam board. **Cover** the area completely and be sure the edges are glued down securely. This will be the background for your constellation! Let it **dry** overnight.

STEP 2

[next day] Using an encyclopedia or the internet, **make notes** about the constellation the teacher assigns your team. **Cut** a strip of paper and **write** your constellation's name. **Pin** this to the top of your background board.

STEP 3

Place a pin in the board for every star in your constellation. If an individual star has a name, **label** it with a slip of paper. Now carefully **stretch** a piece of white thread between the pins to outline your constellation.

STEP 4

Present your constellation to the class. **Tell** how it got its name and other details you discovered in your research. Now **listen** carefully as other teams present their constellations. **Make notes** and **drawings** in your journal.

WHAT HAPPENED?

Sometimes groups of **stars** appear to form **patterns**. Such a grouping is called a **constellation**. Ancient people from various cultures often named constellations for the shapes they saw there. The constellation models you made represent certain portions of Earth's night sky.

If you were on the other side of the galaxy, however, these same stars would form different groupings. Some would be closer; some farther away. Some might not even be visible! The thick band of stars we call the **Milky Way**, for instance, is just the edge of our own **galaxy** as seen from Earth. From another part of the universe, our galaxy might appear as a disk or even a spiral!

WHAT WE LEARNED

1 What constellation did your team research in Step 2? Describe what you discovered about this constellation.

2 How would you locate your constellation in the night sky? Would it require a telescope or a certain time of year? Explain.

3 Did individual stars in your constellation have names?
If so, what were their names or labels?

_____

_____

_____

_____

_____

4 Pick a constellation researched by another team. What did you learn
from their presentation about this constellation?

_____

_____

_____

_____

_____

5 Would your constellation look different from the other side of the
galaxy? Explain your answer.

_____

_____

_____

_____

_____

? CONCLUSION

A constellation is a pattern of stars as seen from Earth. Such patterns would look much different if they were viewed from another part of the galaxy.

FOOD FOR THOUGHT

Genesis 1:16 If you want to see how the night sky looked to people long ago, you have to get out of the cities and towns. Without the competition of man-made lights, each star is crisp, clear, and bright. On a clear summer night, the sky is filled with dazzling brilliance!

This Scripture reminds us that God created the universe. He placed the sun, moon, and stars in their appointed places. Looking at the night sky, we're amazed at the immense creative power it represents. Yet the mighty God who created the entire universe has room in his heart for you! Never forget that God loves you with a love that will outlast the heavens.

JOURNAL My Science Notes

NAME _____

GRAVITY GRABBER

FOCUS Gravitational Fields

OBJECTIVE To explore how gravity affects objects

OVERVIEW Here on Earth, gravity is constantly pulling us downward. What about objects out in space? In this activity, we'll explore gravitational fields by building a model.

WHAT TO DO

STEP 1

Gently **stretch** a sheet of plastic wrap over the top of a one-gallon ice cream bucket. Keep it smooth but not too tight. Use masking tape to **secure** it to the bucket. This plastic sheet represents the deep reaches of outer space.

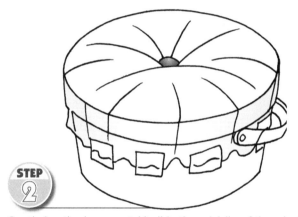

STEP 2

Gently **lay** the large metal ball in the middle of the plastic. This ball represents a huge object in space — something like a star! **Observe** the plastic wrap around the ball and **make note**s about what you see.

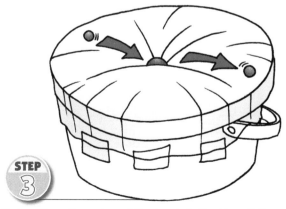

STEP 3

Set a BB on the edge of the bucket. Gently **roll** it past the ball to the other side. **Record** the results. **Repeat** using different paths and speeds. Now **experiment** with the other two sizes of metal balls. **Record** the results.

STEP 4

Review the steps in this activity. **Discuss** how the path of the BB past the ball simulated the force of gravity. **Make notes** about what your team observed. **Share** and **compare** observations with other research teams.

WHAT HAPPENED?

The empty plastic sheet represents an area of **space** with no objects. When you added the large metal ball, it made a dent. The size of the dent represents the object's **gravitational field** — how far it can easily **attract** other objects. It also shows how **gravity** relates to **mass**. A large ball (greater mass) makes a big dent (large gravitational field). A small ball (less mass) makes a small dent (small gravitational field).

The large ball in the middle represents a **star**. Some of the balls you shot went right by the star. They were moving too fast or were too far away to be affected. Other balls were close enough, but still moving too fast. They passed by, but their **direction** and **speed** were changed. (NASA uses this gravitational "slingshot" effect to whip satellites deeper into space.) And some balls were close and slow, so gravity **pulled** them into the star.

WHAT WE LEARNED

1 Compare the plastic wrap in Step 1 with the plastic wrap in Step 2. How are they similar? How are they different?

2 What does the dent around the large ball represent? How did this dent affect the BB in Step 3?

3 What were the three possible paths the BB could have taken? List the factors that would cause it to take each of these paths.

_____

_____

_____

_____

_____

_____

4 Describe how NASA uses the gravity of large planets to extend the range of their satellites.

_____

_____

_____

_____

_____

5 Explain how mass relates to gravity. Give at least one example.

_____

_____

_____

_____

_____

CONCLUSION

The greater the mass of the object, the greater its gravitational field. The gravitational fields of planets affect passing objects in various ways.

FOOD FOR THOUGHT

Ezekiel 33:11 Objects in space can be attracted by a planet's gravity. The closer they get to the planet, the greater the pull. Some objects eventually come too close. They're trapped by the planet's gravitational field and may crash into the planet.

In a similar way, people are attracted by the tricks of Satan. The closer they get to bad companions and worthless amusements, the greater the pull. Before long, they find themselves trapped in a web of sin. Scripture warns us to turn away from such evil. Keep your eyes on Christ, and you can stay far from the pull of the evil one.

JOURNAL My Science Notes

NAME _____

PERSONAL PLANET

FOCUS Earth Structure

OBJECTIVE To explore the layers of the Earth

OVERVIEW How is the Earth made? Is it the same material all the way through? In this activity, we'll explore Earth's structure by making a model.

WHAT TO DO

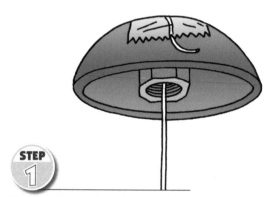

STEP 1

Tie a small metal nut in the middle of a string. This represents the core of the Earth. **Slip** the end of the string through the hole in the popper and **pull** until the nut is even with the popper's bottom edge.

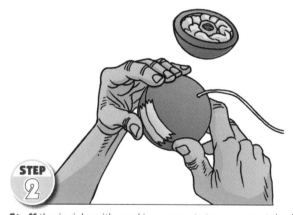

STEP 2

Stuff the inside with packing peanuts to represent the layer next to the core (mostly iron and nickel). The popper is another layer (mostly igneous rock). **Tape** a second popper to the first to make a ball. The seam is the Equator.

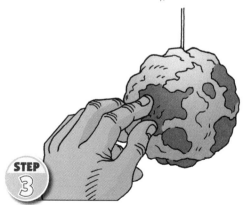

STEP 3

Flatten the yellow, blue, and green clays into very thin layers. **Cover** the ball with yellow clay. This represents the bottom layer of the crust. **Look** at a globe. **Cover** all the yellow with blue clay for oceans; green clay for land.

STEP 4

Review each step in this activity. **Make notes** comparing the thickness of the various layers. **Share** and **compare** observations with your research team.

WHAT HAPPENED?

This **model** represents the relative thickness of Earth's **layers**. The nut represents the inner **core** of the Earth. The packing peanuts represent the outer core. The popper represents the **mantle**. The layers of clay represent the **crust** of Earth.

Scientist believe Earth's core is mostly iron. Because of enormous pressure, the inner portion of the core is solid iron. The outer core is liquid (**molten**) iron.

The mantle is made of **minerals** in a state between molten and solid. These minerals are mostly melted **igneous rock** that scientists call **magma**.

The crust of the Earth (the part you walk on) is relatively **solid**. It has layers of its own, mostly made of rock, soil, sand, and similar materials.

WHAT WE LEARNED

1 Name the three primary parts of the model. How were they similar? How were they different?

_____

_____

_____

_____

_____

_____

2 Name and describe the innermost (center) layer of Earth. What do scientists believe it is composed of? What are its two parts?

_____

_____

_____

_____

_____

_____

3 Name the middle layer of Earth. What is it composed of?
What do scientists call the melted rock?

4 Name and describe the outer layer of Earth. What is it composed of?
How does this layer compare to the other layers?

5 What states of matter are represented in this model?
Explain your answer.

CONCLUSION

The Earth is a series of complicated layers that contain tremendous energy. These layers can be divided into three major sections: the core, the mantle, and the crust.

FOOD FOR THOUGHT

2 Thessalonians 3:6-10 Models are very useful tools for helping us understand the world around us. In this Scripture, Paul writes about the importance of being a good model to others.

Think about the way you treat people around you. Are you being a good model? Does the way you relate to others reflect the love of God? The more time you spend learning about God, the more you'll be able to truly reflect God's character to the world.

JOURNAL My Science Notes

Energy
& MATTER

ENERGY and MATTER

LESSONS 28-36

Energy and Matter

In this section, you'll learn about the different **states** and unique **properties** of **matter**. You'll discover new things about light and sound. You'll explore physical and chemical reactions. Some grades will explore related concepts like circuits, currents, and convection.

BAFFLING BEADS

FOCUS Light Spectrum

OBJECTIVE To explore ultraviolet light

OVERVIEW Light is all around us. But did you know only a small portion of light is visible? In this activity, we'll use special tools to detect the presence of invisible light.

WHAT TO DO

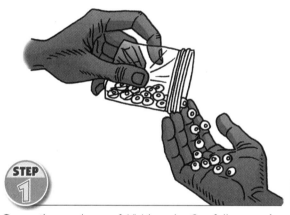

STEP 1

Open the package of UV beads. Carefully **examine** the beads and **describe** them in your journal. Your teacher will explain what UV stands for and where UV rays come from. **Take** good **notes**!

STEP 2

Thread several beads onto a pipe cleaner. **Bend** the pipe cleaner around your wrist to make a wristband. **Step** out into the bright sunlight and **watch** the beads closely. **Record** any changes.

STEP 3

Take the wristband back into the classroom. **Make** a list of beads and colors. **Watch** the wristband for three minutes and **record** any changes. **Place** the wristband in a dark place (inside your desk, etc.) and **leave** it overnight.

STEP 4

[next day] **Look** at the beads again. **Note** any changes. **Review** each step in this activity and **make notes** about what you observed. **Share** and **compare** observations with your research team.

WHAT HAPPENED?

These special beads are made from a material that absorbs the ultraviolet light from sunlight. Ultraviolet light is colorless and invisible, but the beads help indicate its presence. After they've absorbed the light, they begin radiating (releasing) this light. Variations in the material the beads are made from cause the ultraviolet light to show up as different colors.

A rainbow shows you all the colors of visible light. But once you pass violet, the frequency (vibration rate) of light is too fast for your eyes to see. In fact, that's where ultraviolet light gets its name: ultra means "greater than" so ultra-violet means light whose frequency is greater than that of violet light!

WHAT WE LEARNED

1 Compare the beads in Step 1 with those in Step 2.
How were they similar? How were the light sources different?

_____

_____

_____

_____

_____

_____

_____

2 How many beads were on your wristband?
How many colors were represented?

_____

_____

_____

_____

_____

_____

3 What combination created the colors in Step 3?
How is this similar or different from a rainbow?

_____

_____

_____

_____

_____

_____

4 Describe the beads in Step 4 (no light). What happened to the color?

_____

_____

_____

_____

_____

_____

5 Based on what you've learned, would your classroom be a good place
to get a large dose of ultraviolet light? Explain your answer.

_____

_____

_____

_____

_____

_____

CONCLUSION

Only a portion of the light spectrum is visible to the human eye. Invisible forms, like ultraviolet, can be detected with special tools. Light energy can be absorbed and released.

FOOD FOR THOUGHT

Psalm 27:1 When there was no light, the beads looked much the same — dull and featureless. But when they were placed in strong sunlight, they began to absorb ultraviolet light. They absorbed so much that they began to radiate that light back as color. As long as they continued to absorb light, the beads could really shine!

In this Scripture, David reminds us that God is the ultimate source of light. Like the beads, our lives can be pretty dull and featureless. But when we open our hearts to God, we begin to absorb his great love. As our lives are filled, we begin to radiate God's great love to others. But remember, this process can only continue if we stay close to God!

JOURNAL   My Science Notes

SOUND SEEKER

FOCUS   Sound

OBJECTIVE   To explore how sound is made

OVERVIEW   Our sense of hearing is very important. But what causes sound? In this activity, we'll create a device to explore how sound is made.

WHAT TO DO

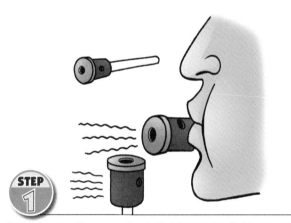

STEP 1

Remove the film container's lid. **Push** the PVC pipe about half way through the large hole in the bottom of the container. **Put** the lid back on. **Blow** across the small hole in the container's side. **Record** the results.

STEP 2

Remove the container's lid. **Stretch** a piece of plastic wrap over the opening and **secure** it with the lid. **Pull** the pipe back slightly (but not out of the container). **Blow** across the small hole again. **Record** the results.

STEP 3

Gently **push** the pipe into the container until it barely touches the plastic. **Blow** across the small hole again. If you don't hear a noise, **move** the pipe slightly using more or less air, or **tighten** the plastic. **Record** the results.

STEP 4

Review each step in this activity. **Make notes** about what conditions made the noisemaker work or not work. **Share** and **compare** observations with your research team.

WHAT HAPPENED?

Sound is produced by a sequence of events. It begins with some form of energy. The energy causes something to move causing vibrations (called waves). The waves make the air move, helping transmit the vibration to a device capable of detecting it.

In this activity, your lungs provided the energy to move air rapidly across the opening. This caused the plastic to vibrate, creating sound waves. The sound waves vibrated the air in the tube, amplifying the sound so your ears could detect it!

Notice that changing the length of the pipe changed the rate of vibration (also known as frequency). The adjustment in vibration rates changed the sound produced.

WHAT WE LEARNED

1 Describe what you heard in Step 1 and Step 2. How were the sounds similar? How were they different?

_____

_____

_____

_____

_____

_____

2 Describe what you heard in Step 3. How was it similar to sounds heard in the other steps? How was it different?

_____

_____

_____

_____

_____

_____

3 Describe the steps necessary to produce sound.

_____

_____

_____

_____

_____

_____

_____

4 Based on what you've learned, what are some factors that might affect how loud a sound is?

_____

_____

_____

_____

_____

_____

_____

5 Think about a band or orchestra you've heard. Choose three instruments. Based on what you've learned, explain why they produce different sounds.

_____

_____

_____

_____

_____

_____

_____

CONCLUSION

To create sound, energy must produce vibration which leads to air movement. The rate of vibration is known as frequency. Frequency has an effect on a sound's pitch.

FOOD FOR THOUGHT

Psalm 95:1-2 In this activity, we discovered the ingredients of sound: energy, vibration, and air movement. The device you made put those all together to produce . . . well, not exactly music . . . but certainly a joyful noise!

Humans are certainly inclined to be noisy creatures, but the kind of noise we make is up to us. This Scripture talks about singing and making music to worship God. It's only one of many such verses in Scripture. Creating sounds of praise is a great way to exercise this part of our nature. Think of God's great love and make joyful, happy sounds for your creator!

JOURNAL My Science Notes

LIQUID LITERACY

LESSON 30

FOCUS Properties of Light

OBJECTIVE To explore how fluids affect light

OVERVIEW Certain liquids are easy to see through. But are you seeing what's really there? In this activity, we'll use "reading fluid" to find out!

WHAT TO DO

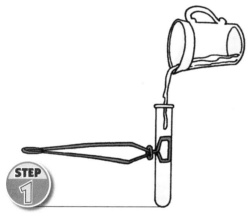

STEP 1

Watch as your teacher fills your test tube with "reading fluid." **Seal** the tube by putting the stopper firmly in the opening. **Observe** the liquid and **make notes** about what you see.

STEP 2

Write BOB on a sheet of paper in letters about 1/2 inch tall. Be sure to use all capitals. Now **write** DAVE about one inch below it. The "reading fluid" will help you read one name, but not the other! **Predict** why this might be.

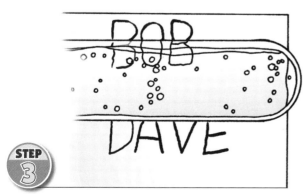

STEP 3

Hold the tube about one inch above DAVE. **Look** through the tube and **make notes** about what you see. Now **repeat** this step with the name BOB. **Record** the results.

STEP 4

Review each step in this activity. **Discuss** what the "reading fluid" in the tube might be. **Make notes** about the different results in Step 3. **Share** and **compare** observations with your research team.

WHAT HAPPENED?

The "reading fluid" we used for this activity was ordinary water. Clear water is easy to see through (**transparent**), but it also causes **light** to slow down. It's like running through a field of tall grass compared to running on the gym floor. The thick grass (high **density**) slows your movement.

When high density materials like water or glass slow light down, they cause the light to **refract** (bend). In Step 3, you used the tube like a **lens**. The light reaching your eyes from the **image** slowed down so much that it caused the image to **invert** (flip).

Now here's the trick. Since the capital letters O and B look the same right side up or upside down, you could read "BOB," but you couldn't read "DAVE" because the A and V were inverted!

WHAT WE LEARNED

1 Describe the liquid you put into the test tube in Step 1. What effect did this liquid have on light?

_____

_____

_____

_____

_____

_____

2 What did you predict in Step 2? How did this prediction reflect what actually happened?

_____

_____

_____

_____

_____

_____

3 What is the process of bending light called?
How is this process helpful in correcting eye problems?

_____

_____

_____

_____

_____

_____

4 Explain why one name was easy to read through the tube of water and the other wasn't.

_____

_____

_____

_____

_____

_____

_____

5 Based on what you've learned, explain why Native Americans had to understand the relationship between water and light to hunt fish with a bow.

_____

_____

_____

_____

_____

_____

CONCLUSION

Some materials can slow light, causing it to refract (bend). Lenses help control the degree of refraction. Certain kinds of lenses use refraction to produce an inverted image.

FOOD FOR THOUGHT

Proverbs 27:19 All vision is based on light reflecting off a surface to your eyes. But as we saw in this activity, there are times when things interfere with an accurate reflection. Often we need to know more in order to understand whether what we're seeing is the "real thing" or an illusion.

A good mirror shows you an accurate reflection of your face. However, this Scripture reminds us that outward appearance doesn't always show what's inside. The "real you" is shown by the kind of friends you choose and the way you treat others. When God is in your heart, his love can shine out for all to see!

JOURNAL My Science Notes

_____

_____

_____

_____

_____

_____

_____

_____

_____

_____

_____

_____

_____

_____

_____

_____

_____

_____

_____

NAME _____

PERIODIC PUZZLE

FOCUS   Periodic Table

OBJECTIVE   To explore the periodic table

OVERVIEW   Everything around us is made of different elements. How do these elements relate to each other? In this activity, we'll explore how scientists organize this information.

WHAT TO DO

STEP 1

Remove the *Periodic Table Puzzle Pieces* page from the back of your worktext. **Cut out** every item. Carefully **examine** the elements with your research team. **Discuss** different ways you might sort and arrange them.

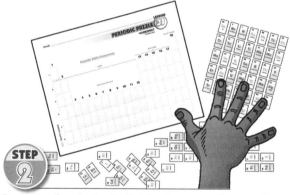

STEP 2

Remove the *Periodic Table Framework* page from the back of your worktext. **Place** it on your work surface and **arrange** the elements beside it in numeric order. (This will make them easy to locate.)

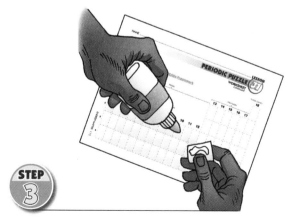

STEP 3

Remove the *Periodic Table Reference* page from the back of your worktext. Use this as a guide. Now **find** the *Puzzle Piece* from Step 1 that has the atomic number 1 (Hydrogen). **Glue** it in the correct spot on the *Framework* from Step 2.

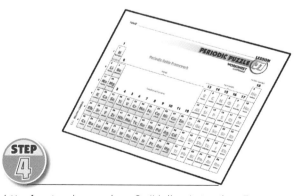

STEP 4

Attach atomic number 2 (Helium) to the *Framework*. **Continue** until all the elements are attached. **Compare** your table to the reference page. **Make notes** about similarities and differences. **Share** and **compare** observations with your research team.

WHAT HAPPENED?

As early as 400 B.C., the Greeks referred to small particles of **matter** as **elements**. They believed there were four primary elements — earth, fire, air, and water. Over the centuries, understanding of elements increased greatly. Then in the 1800s, scientists began to notice that some elements behaved alike. Many scientists contributed to the organization of these elements into groups of various kinds based on different characteristics, eventually leading to what we know today as the **Periodic Table**.

The modern Periodic Table is based on an element's **atomic number**. Columns are called **families** or **groups**. They're numbered one to eighteen from left to right. Rows are called **periods**. They're numbered one to six from top to bottom. The periodic table we constructed doesn't include every element (there are 94 natural elements), but it does provide a good representation for study. The actual periodic table is much bigger, and even includes artificial elements engineered by man.

WHAT WE LEARNED

1 Describe the history of the word "element." What did the ancient Greeks believe? How does that compare to our understanding?

_____

_____

_____

_____

_____

_____

_____

2 What are the columns on the Periodic Table called? How are they numbered and arranged?

_____

_____

_____

_____

_____

_____

_____

3 What are the rows on the Periodic Table called? How are they numbered and arranged?

_____

_____

_____

_____

_____

_____

4 On your table, what element is in period 4, column 2? What element is in period 6, column 11? What element is in period 2, column 14?

_____

_____

_____

_____

_____

_____

5 Over the years, the Periodic Table has seen changes, additions, and improvements, including a three-dimensional version introduced in 1994. Why might a tool like this change over time?

_____

_____

_____

_____

_____

_____

CONCLUSION

The elements that make up all matter have been organized into a chart called the Periodic Table. This chart organizes elements based on their atomic number and chemical properties.

FOOD FOR THOUGHT

Genesis 2:7 Science has shown us that the elements our bodies are made from are also found in rocks, water, plants, animals — virtually everything around us! The interactions between these different elements in all their various combinations is what science is all about.

But centuries before the first scientist figured out that elements are the basic building blocks of matter, Scripture talked about man being formed "from the dust of the ground." So what's the difference between you and a stone? You have a mind and a soul — put there by the Creator himself! How should you use this precious gift? Read Matthew 22:37 for the answer.

 JOURNAL   My Science Notes

_____

_____

_____

_____

_____

_____

_____

_____

_____

_____

_____

_____

_____

_____

_____

_____

_____

_____

_____

NAME _____

CIRCUIT TESTER

FOCUS Electricity

OBJECTIVE To explore circuits, insulators, and conductors

OVERVIEW We use electricity every day. But how does it work, and what makes this powerful force safe to use? In this activity, we'll explore its characteristics by building a circuit tester.

WHAT TO DO

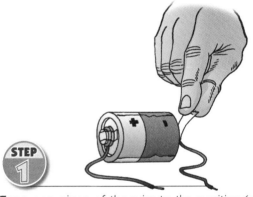

STEP 1

Tape one piece of the wire to the positive (+) terminal of the D cell battery. **Tape** a second piece of wire to the negative (-) terminal. **Check** to make sure the wires are taped securely. Don't let the ends touch!

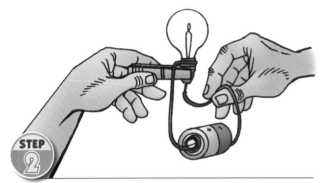

STEP 2

Wrap the bare end of one wire around the threads of the light bulb. **Grab** the bulb with the clothespin to secure. Now **touch** the bare end of the other wire to the bottom of the bulb. **Record** the results.

STEP 3

Touch the bulb to one end of a paperclip. Now **touch** the wire to the other end of the paperclip. **Record** the results. **Repeat** using a piece of paper, then a penny, then a piece of plastic. **Record** the results.

STEP 4

Review the four parts of Step 3. **Predict** why the results were different. **Share** and **compare** observations with your research team.

WHAT HAPPENED?

The **electricity** in your battery came from a **chemical reaction**. But the **electrons** couldn't get out of the battery to provide **energy** without a path to follow. When you touched the wire to the bulb, you created a path that allowed electrons to flow. This is called a **closed circuit**. Removing the wire broke the path, creating an **open circuit**.

Anything that allows electricity to flow from one place to another (like copper wire) is called a **conductor**. Anything that stops the flow of electricity, keeping it isolated (like the plastic coating on the wire) is called an **insulator**.

A **switch** controls electricity by **opening** or **closing** a circuit. You use a switch every time you turn out the lights. Most electrical devices have a switch of some sort.

WHAT WE LEARNED

1 Describe the difference between an open circuit and a closed circuit.

_____

_____

_____

_____

_____

_____

2 Describe what happened in Step 2. What kind of circuit did this represent? What indicated it was working?

_____

_____

_____

_____

_____

_____

3 Explain what happened as you tested each item in Step 3. Which were conductors? Which were insulators?

_____

_____

_____

_____

_____

_____

4 What is the purpose of a switch in a circuit? Name three common devices that use switches.

_____

_____

_____

_____

_____

_____

5 What was the electricity source for this activity? How is this current different from household current? Why should you never experiment with household current?

_____

_____

_____

_____

_____

_____

_____

CONCLUSION

A connected path for electricity is a closed circuit. A disconnected path is an open circuit. Materials that carry current are conductors. Materials that don't carry current are insulators. A switch can open and close circuits.

FOOD FOR THOUGHT

John 14:6 The bulb couldn't access the energy in the battery until it was connected. It didn't matter if the day was sunny or dark with clouds — as long as the bulb was firmly connected, it kept burning brightly. But when the connection was broken, the light faded away.

This Scripture reminds us there is only one way to connect to God's power — through Jesus! As long as we are connected to him, the life-giving power continues to flow. It doesn't matter if times are good, or our world is full of sorrow and pain. As long as we're connected to the Father, we'll continue to be filled with his light.

JOURNAL   My Science Notes

_____

_____

_____

_____

_____

_____

_____

_____

_____

_____

_____

_____

_____

_____

_____

_____

_____

_____

_____

_____

_____

SHIFTING SULFATE

FOCUS States of Matter

OBJECTIVE To compare physical and chemical change

OVERVIEW Change is constantly happening all around you. In science, there are two basic kinds of change: physical and chemical. In this activity, we'll explore one of these changes.

WHAT TO DO

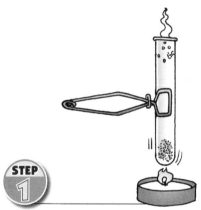

STEP 1

Pour a few crystals of blue copper sulfate into a test tube, barely covering the bottom. **Light** the candle and **hold** the test tube over the flame for 60 seconds. **Record** the results.

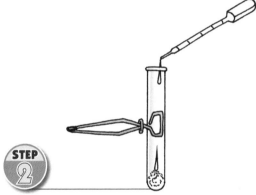

STEP 2

Allow the test tube to cool completely. (If the tube is not cool for this step, it will break!) Now **add** a small drop of water to the crystals. **Record** the results.

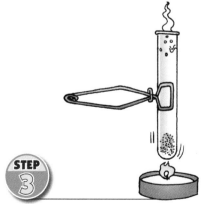

STEP 3

Relight the candle and **hold** the test tube over the flame again. **Heat** until something happens. **Record** the results. **Allow** the test tube to cool completely, then **dispose** of the crystals as your teacher directs.

STEP 4

Review each step in this activity. **Make notes** and drawings about what you observed. **Share** and **compare** observations with your research team.

WHAT HAPPENED?

A **physical change** affects the **form** of a material, but it's still the same **substance** when you're through. (A good example is **freezing** water to make ice cubes. The form changes, but it's still water.) A **chemical change** creates a **different** substance from the one you started with. (A good example is **burning** a piece of wood. Once it's burned, it's no longer wood.)

The copper sulfate you used is a **hydrate**, which means it has water attached. The **heat energy** drove the water out, resulting in a color change. When you put water back in, there was another color change. But neither of these changes created a different substance. It was still copper sulfate when you were done.

WHAT WE LEARNED

1 **Describe what happened to the crystals in Step 1. What color were they before heating? What color were they after heating?**

_____

_____

_____

_____

_____

_____

2 **Describe what happened to the crystals in Step 2. What color were they before adding water? What color were they after the water was added?**

_____

_____

_____

_____

_____

_____

3 Describe what happened in Step 3.
Compare this with Step 1 and Step 2.

_____

_____

_____

_____

_____

_____

4 Explain the difference between chemical change and physical change.

_____

_____

_____

_____

_____

_____

_____

5 Based on what you've learned, give an example of a chemical change and an example of a physical change. Explain your answers.

_____

_____

_____

_____

_____

_____

❓ CONCLUSION

A physical change affects the form of a material, but it's still the same substance. A chemical change results in a different substance from the one you started with. Both changes involve energy.

📖 FOOD FOR THOUGHT

1 Samuel 10:6 This Scripture tells about the anointing of Saul by the prophet Samuel. Saul was changed by God's power, and he went on to become a great ruler of Israel. Unfortunately, as he grew older, Saul began to trust more and more in his own power. Eventually, this great king turned away from God.

You saw some significant changes inside that test tube, but they were only physical changes. No matter what form it took, the material was still copper sulfate. You can make great changes by allowing God's power in your life. But don't make Saul's mistake! Spend time every day renewing your contact with God and letting his power work through you.

📖 JOURNAL   My Science Notes

NAME _____

COOL COIN

FOCUS Conductors

OBJECTIVE Explore how heat is transferred

OVERVIEW It takes oxygen, fuel, and heat to make a fire. Remove any one of these and there's no fire. In this activity, we'll explore how heat is transferred.

WHAT TO DO

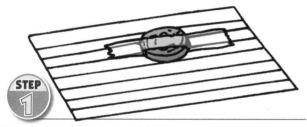

STEP 1

Place a candle in the middle of an aluminum pan. **Tape** a dime "heads up" in the middle of an index card. **Predict** what might happen if you hold the card over the candle flame.

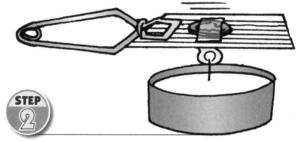

STEP 2

Place the card in your test tube holder. **Hold** it so the "head" faces you. **Light** the candle and gently **move** the card back and forth over the flame. It should get hot, but don't let it catch on fire!

STEP 3

Allow the dime to cool completely. (This may take some time!) Once the dime is cool, **remove** it from the card. **Look** carefully at the area of the card that was covered by the dime. **Record** your observations.

STEP 4

Review each step in this activity. **Make notes** about what happened and why. **Share** and **compare** observations with your research team.

WHAT HAPPENED?

There are three sides to a **fire triangle**; oxygen, fuel, and heat. There was plenty of **oxygen** in the air, the paper provided the **fuel**, and a match has sufficient **heat** to start a fire. If all three parts of the fire triangle were balanced, the fire should have scorched the card evenly.

Yet when you removed the dime, you found an unburned area beneath it! This occurred because the metal in the dime is a great **conductor** of **heat energy**. It **absorbed** the heat, keeping it from **burning** the card.

Of course, this works both ways. Over time the dime could absorb so much heat that it might *start* a fire if you set it on a fresh card!

WHAT WE LEARNED

1 **What are the three "sides" of a fire triangle? What does removing any one of these do?**

_____

_____

_____

_____

_____

_____

_____

2 **Describe what happened to the card in Step 2.**

_____

_____

_____

_____

_____

_____

3 Why wasn't the area beneath the dime scorched?
What did the metal do to the heat energy?

_____

_____

_____

_____

_____

_____

4 In this activity, the dime served as a conductor.
Give at least three examples of metal conducting heat.

_____

_____

_____

_____

_____

_____

5 Based on what you've learned, would a metal wall provide good
protection from a fire? Explain your answer.

_____

_____

_____

_____

_____

_____

CONCLUSION

Fire requires three things: oxygen, fuel, and heat. If any of these are removed, a fire can't occur. Heat energy can be absorbed and transferred by materials called conductors.

FOOD FOR THOUGHT

2 Samuel 22:31 You may have been surprised that the flame didn't scorch the entire index card. There was a dime-size area of safety. By absorbing the heat, the coin provided a shield for the paper, keeping it safe from harm.

This Scripture reminds us that God will shield those who stand behind him. This song of David is full of protective words like rock, refuge, fortress, and shield. Even though we're surrounded by a world full of evil, God keeps our souls safe from harm. Spend time learning to trust him better and let God be your shield!

JOURNAL My Science Notes

NAME _____

BURNING STEEL

FOCUS Chemical Change

OBJECTIVE To explore how surface area affects oxidation

OVERVIEW Some things burn and some things don't. Can you burn steel with a match? In this activity, we'll explore how surface area affects the answer.

WHAT TO DO

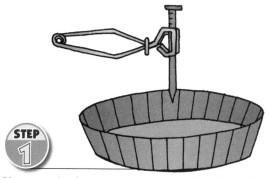

STEP 1

Place an aluminum pan on your work surface. **Put** the nail in the test tube holder. **Predict** what will happen if you try to burn the nail with a match.

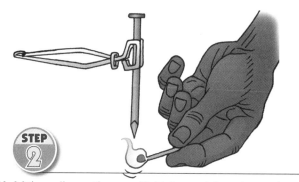

STEP 2

Hold the nail over the pan. **Light** the match and try to **burn** the nail. **Record** the results. Now **stretch** some steel wool into a loose bunch about three inches long. **Predict** what will happen if you try to burn the steel wool.

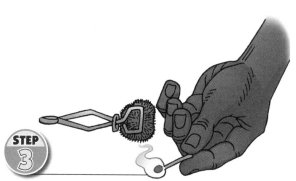

STEP 3

Grab the steel wool with the test tube holder and **hold** it over the pan. (Make sure there are no flammable materials near the pan, including your hair!) **Light** the match and try to burn the steel wool. **Record** the results.

STEP 4

Review each step in this activity. **Make note**s about what happened and why it may have occurred. **Share** and **compare** observations with your research team.

WHAT HAPPENED?

Burning is a **chemical change** (called **oxidation**). A chemical change results in a different **substance** than the substance you started with.

But why will steel wool burn, but not a nail? The answer has to do with **surface area** — the amount of a material directly exposed to oxygen (in the air). The nail is **dense** and compact, but the steel wool is thin and spread out. Steel wool exposes thousands of times more surface to the air.

For a fire to occur, iron **atoms** had to **combine** with oxygen atoms. The small surface area of the nail allowed only a limited number of iron atoms to touch the air. But the steel wool's surface area allowed thousands of times more iron atoms access to the oxygen. Add a **heat** source (the match), and the result is a flash fire!

WHAT WE LEARNED

1
What did you predict in Step 1?
How did this prediction reflect what actually happened?

_____

_____

_____

_____

_____

_____

_____

2
What did you predict in Step 2?
How did this prediction reflect what actually happened?

_____

_____

_____

_____

_____

_____

_____

3 Describe what happened in Step 3.

_____

_____

_____

_____

_____

_____

4 Explain why the steel in the nail didn't burn, but the steel in the steel wool did.

_____

_____

_____

_____

_____

_____

5 If one piece of paper is smashed into a tight ball, and an identical piece of paper is shredded into tiny pieces, which paper would burn the easiest? Explain your answer.

_____

_____

_____

_____

_____

_____

CONCLUSION

When a substance combines with oxygen, the change is called oxidation. Some oxidation is rapid (like burning) and some oxidation is slow (like rusting). However, both involve a chemical process.

FOOD FOR THOUGHT

Matthew 13:3-8 When you tried to burn the nail, nothing happened. You probably weren't surprised. When you tried to burn the steel wool, you got a completely different reaction! Preparing a material differently can significantly change its properties.

It's the same with our hearts. When we prepare with worship and prayer, God finds our hearts a great place to light the fire of love. But when we don't take time for God, our hearts can become hard and unreceptive. Why not spend some quality time with God this week? Let God's power set your heart on fire with heavenly love.

JOURNAL My Science Notes

FLOWERS & FUMES

FOCUS Indicators

OBJECTIVE To explore how indicators work

OVERVIEW Sometimes things aren't what they seem. There are many substances that our eyes can't detect. In this activity, we'll explore how an indicator can help us see what's really there!

WHAT TO DO

STEP 1

Pour about an inch of ammonium hydroxide into a paper cup. (Keep it away from eyes, noses, etc.) Carefully **stretch** a piece of plastic wrap over the cup and **secure** it with a rubber band.

STEP 2

Carefully **cut** a slit in the plastic. **Dampen** the flower by quickly dipping it in a cup of water. **Shake** off any excess. Now **slip** the flower through the plastic and **hold** it just above the liquid. Don't let it touch the liquid!

STEP 3

Observe what happens to the flower and **record** the results. Now **remove** the flower and **blow** on it gently. **Record** the results. **Repeat** until everyone has had a turn.

STEP 4

Review each step in this activity. **Make notes** and drawings about what happened. **Share** and **compare** observations with your research team.

WHAT HAPPENED?

Even though it looked clean, your flower had been soaked in **phenolphthalein**. Phenolphthalein is a chemical called an **indicator**. It doesn't change colors when there's an **acid** around, but it turns pink when a **base** is near. The **ammonium hydroxide** in your cup was giving off **fumes** (gas). Since these fumes contained a base (ammonia), the flower turned pink when the fumes touched it!

Then in Step 3, you began to blow on the flower. The ammonia began to **evaporate**. In addition, your breath contains **carbon dioxide**, and this **reacted** with the water to create a mild acid. With no more base present, and the addition of the acid from your breath, the flower changed back to white.

WHAT WE LEARNED

1 What was the purpose of the plastic cover on the cup in Step 1? What were you trying to contain?

_____

_____

_____

_____

_____

_____

_____

2 Describe what the flower looked like in Step 1. How did its appearance change in Step 2?

_____

_____

_____

_____

_____

_____

_____

3 Describe what happened to the flower in Step 3.
How did its appearance change?

_____

_____

_____

_____

_____

_____

4 Why did the flower change colors?
Describe each step in the process.

_____

_____

_____

_____

_____

_____

5 How might the results have been affected if the ammonium hydroxide
had been sitting in an uncovered cup for a week. Explain your answer.

_____

_____

_____

_____

_____

_____

CONCLUSION

Indicators can be used to detect the presence of an acid or a base. Different kinds of indicators are used for different purposes.

FOOD FOR THOUGHT

Genesis 2:7 In this activity, you saw an amazing change. The ammonia fumes made the flower's colors suddenly come alive! Everything that was dull before was instantly bright with color.

This Scripture tells how God gathered materials from the Earth, formed a body, and breathed into it the breath of life. In one amazing moment, man became a living creature. Spending time with our creator God has a similar effect on our souls. The more we're filled with God's love, the more alive we become!

JOURNAL My Science Notes

_____

_____

_____

_____

_____

_____

_____

_____

_____

_____

_____

_____

_____

_____

_____

_____

_____

_____

Appendix

PREDATOR OR PREY
WORKSHEET

Mountain Lion
(Puma concolor)
(Felis concolor)

Eland
(Taurotragus oryx)

Chinook Salmon
(Oncorhynchus tshawytscha)

Prairie Dog
(Cynomys leucurus)

Lion
(Panthera leo)

Eastern Cottontail
(Sylvilagus floridanus)

Grizzly Bear
(Ursus arctos)

Wild Boar
(Sus scrofa)

Tiger
(Panthera tigris tigris)

Gray Wolf
(Canis lupus)

Red Fox
(Vulpes vulpes)

White-tailed Deer
(Odocoileus virginianus)

NAME _____

FOAM FLYER
WORKSHEET

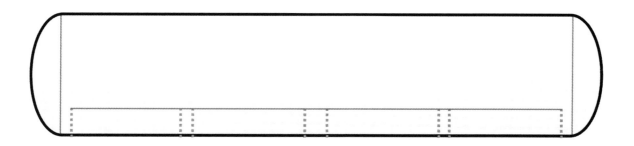

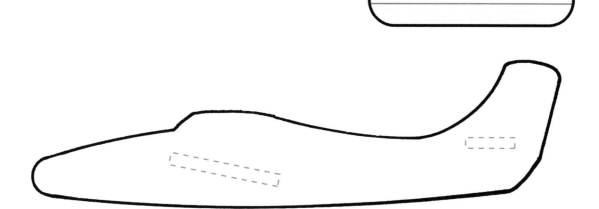

———————	**Cut Out**
– – – – –	**Cut Through**
———————	**Score**

NAME _____

CLASSIFIED CLOUDS
WORKSHEET

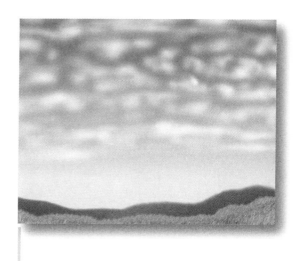

LESSON 31

PERIODIC PUZZLE
WORKSHEET

Periodic Table Reference

Noble Gasses

Nonmetals

Metals

Transitional Elements

1	2	3	4	5	6	7	8	9	10	11	12	13	14	15	16	17	18
1 **H** hydrogen																	2 **He** helium
3 **Li** lithium	4 **Be** beryllium											5 **B** boron	6 **C** carbon	7 **N** nitrogen	8 **O** oxygen	9 **F** fluorine	10 **Ne** neon
11 **Na** sodium	12 **Mg** magnesium											13 **Al** aluminium	14 **Si** silicon	15 **P** phosphorus	16 **S** sulphur	17 **Cl** chlorine	18 **Ar** argon
19 **K** potassium	20 **Ca** calcium	21 **Sc** scandium	22 **Ti** titanium	23 **V** vanadium	24 **Cr** chromium	25 **Mn** manganese	26 **Fe** iron	27 **Co** cobalt	28 **Ni** nickel	29 **Cu** copper	30 **Zn** zinc	31 **Ga** gallium	32 **Ge** germanium	33 **As** arsenic	34 **Se** selenium	35 **Br** bromine	36 **Kr** krypton
37 **Rb** rubidium	38 **Sr** strontium	39 **Y** yttrium	40 **Zr** zirconium	41 **Nb** niobium	42 **Mo** molybdenum	43 **Tc** technetium	44 **Ru** ruthenium	45 **Rh** rhodium	46 **Pd** palladium	47 **Ag** silver	48 **Cd** cadmium	49 **In** indium	50 **Sn** tin	51 **Sb** antimony	52 **Te** tellurium	53 **I** iodine	54 **Xe** xenon
55 **Cs** caesium	56 **Ba** barium	71 **Lu** lutetium	72 **Hf** hafnium	73 **Ta** tantalum	74 **W** tungsten	75 **Re** rhenium	76 **Os** osmium	77 **Ir** iridium	78 **Pt** platinum	79 **Au** gold	80 **Hg** mercury	81 **Tl** thallium	82 **Pb** lead	83 **Bi** bismuth	84 **Po** polonium	85 **At** astatine	86 **Rn** radon

PERIODIC PUZZLE

WORKSHEET
Continued

Periodic Table Puzzle Pieces

NAME

36 **Kr** krypton	2 **He** helium	17 **Cl** chlorine	86 **Rn** radon	85 **At** astatine	48 **Cd** cadmium
80 **Hg** mercury	6 **C** carbon	7 **N** nitrogen	8 **O** oxygen	16 **S** sulphur	84 **Po** polonium
76 **Os** osmium	77 **Ir** iridium	51 **Sb** antimony	78 **Pt** platinum	46 **Pd** palladium	79 **Au** gold
18 **Ar** argon	34 **Se** selenium	28 **Ni** nickel	29 **Cu** copper	30 **Zn** zinc	35 **Br** bromine
26 **Fe** iron	27 **Co** cobalt	45 **Rh** rhodium	52 **Te** tellurium	44 **Ru** ruthenium	9 **F** fluorine
32 **Ge** germanium	10 **Ne** neon	39 **Y** yttrium	°47 **Ag** silver	°53 **I** iodine	°55 **Cs** caesium
43 **Tc** technetium	25 **Mn** manganese	54 **Xe** xenon	°42 **Mo** molybdenum	°83 **Bi** bismuth	°75 **Re** rhenium
82 **Pb** lead	41 **Nb** niobium	19 **K** potassium	°81 **Tl** thallium	°74 **W** tungsten	°14 **Si** silicon
31 **Ga** gallium	22 **Ti** titanium	20 **Ca** calcium	°12 **Mg** magnesium	°13 **Al** aluminium	°73 **Ta** tantalum
1 **H** hydrogen	3 **Li** lithium	5 **B** boron	°23 **V** vanadium	°37 **Rb** rubidium	°15 **P** phosphorus
4 **Be** beryllium	21 **Sc** scandium	49 **In** indium	°33 **As** arsenic	°72 **Hf** hafnium	°56 **Ba** barium
50 **Sn** tin	24 **Cr** chromium	11 **Na** sodium	°40 **Zr** zirconium	°38 **Sr** strontium	°71 **Lu** lutetium

NAME

PERIODIC PUZZLE

Periodic Table Framework

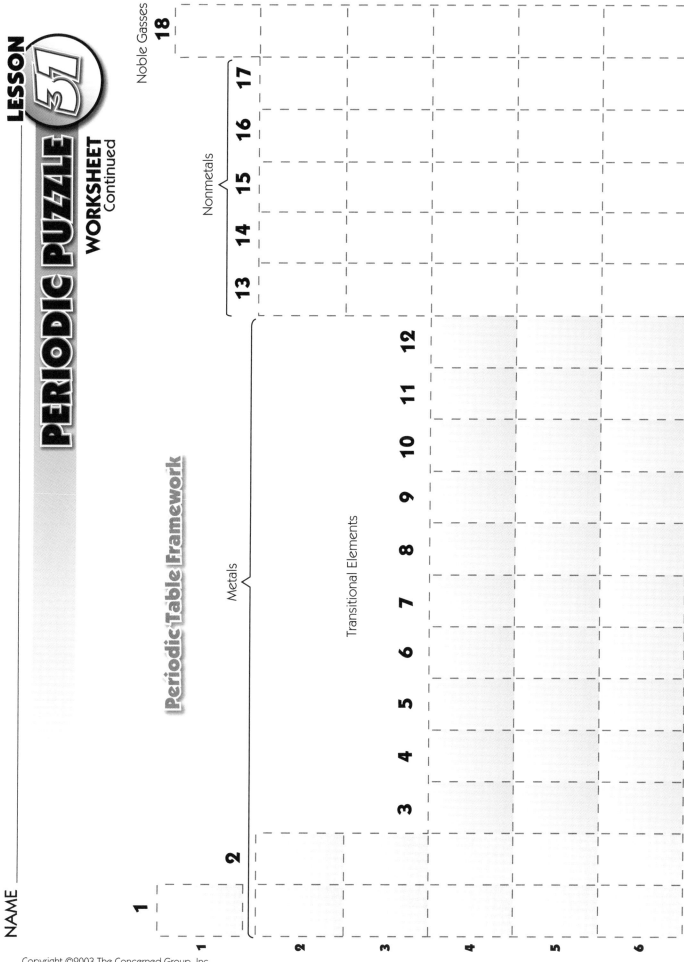

Noble Gasses

Nonmetals

Metals

Transitional Elements

NAME _____

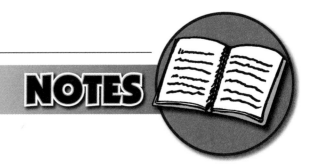